On Screen Acting

An Introduction to the Art of Acting for the Screen

EDWARD AND JEAN PORTER DMYTRYK

FOCAL PRESS
Boston • London

Focal Press is an imprint of Butterworth Publishers.

Library of Congress Cataloging in Publication Data

Dmytryk, Edward.
  On screen acting.

  1. Moving-picture acting.   I. Dmytryk, Jean Porter.
II. Title.
PN1995.D57 1984   791.43'028   84–13592
ISBN 0–240–51739–3

Butterworth Publishers
80 Montvale Avenue
Stoneham, MA 02180

10 9 8 7 6 5 4 3 2

Printed in the United States of America

Contents

Introduction

Acting is almost certainly the oldest of the arts. Long before he painted the walls of his caves, primitive man staged initiation ceremonies and "counted coup," much as the American Indian did well into the nineteenth century. Counting coup, the recital of one's courage and prowess in battle or at the hunt, often involved the most strenuous and hyperbolic (today we would call it hammy) kind of acting.

Before the advent of the written word, the storyteller was perhaps the tribe's most treasured asset; he was its geneologist, historian, and entertainer. He enjoyed protection and privileges far beyond those of most of his community. After all, even the chief was expendable, with a covey of ambitious citizens ready to take his place, but a good storyteller was (and still is) hard to find. Quite obviously, the better the presentation the better the story, and the better the acting the better the presentation. The verbal storyteller's art has persisted to the present era, surviving even in some relatively sophisticated modern societies.

The invention of the alphabet led to more formal and more artful techniques, all of which have been reported and described by a thousand critics, historians, and practitioners in thousands of books, which spares me the necessity of detailing them here.

Until recently, all acting performances, from the warrior singing his own praises, through the bard singing those of others, to the modern actor breathing life into some playwright's offering

of suspense, action, or high drama, had two things in common—
they told a story, and they had an immediate audience.

Then came the movies and the capability of recording performances for future viewing. For the first time in the long history
of dramatic art the performer was divorced from his audience.
To be sure, the audience was still indispensable, but it congre-
gated somewhere down the line. In fact, the performer himself
could also be a part of his own audience. But now he had to work
alone, removed from the encouragement, the warm personal satisfaction he had once derived from his rapport with his auditors.

And that, in a nutshell, is the reason for a special work on
acting for the screen. It is the absence of audience rapport plus
its corollary—the freedom to place the actor at any arbitrary
distance from the eventual viewer—that makes screen acting a
different art, a more honest art, and an art that has its own premises and its own techniques. In the succeeding pages we describe
what those premises are and analyze the techniques that spring
from them. We do that not as teachers, but from the standpoints
of the director and the performing artist.

Actress Jean Porter talks to Jack Dawn.

1

The Interview

Interviews—what budding artist can avoid them? No director will risk using an untried actor,* even one with some professional experience, without first interviewing him. Even if there is existing material that can be viewed—a test or a bit of some previously shot film—a personal interview is desirable, if not mandatory.

The interview is probably the first contact between actor and director, and first impressions are important. Quite obviously, since the director is "bestowing" and the actor is "receiving," it is the impression the actor makes on the director that is important, not vice versa.

Every director has his own prejudices, his own way of making judgments, but there are a number of factors with nearly universal application. Any young actor who neglects to consider such factors is not giving himself half a fair chance. For instance, if possible (and it usually is), he should get as much information as he can about the director in question. He should then be able, well short of obvious flattery or downright boot licking, to present the side of his personality that will most positively impress his

---

*In a profession that has been quite free of sexist prejudice for at least the last hundred years, it has become common to use the word "actor" to apply to thespians of either sex, and we so use it in this book. The use of the pronouns "he," "him," or "his" will, we hope, be graciously taken as applying equally to male or female actors—and directors.

interlocutor. It's fine to be youself, but don't let it all come out in a brief interview; the "self" you present may not be the "self" he will want to see on the screen or work with on the set. And for God's sake don't, in an effort at ego establishment, pontificate on the low quality of films in general. He may consider your remarks as youthful impertinence rather than as mature, valid judgments of his profession.

Let us now get to specifics. Let us assume a young actress has stepped into my office for her first interview. I know that her knees are a bit wobbly and her palms are sweating, and I will do everything I can to make her feel at ease. This is not a purely unselfish exercise—I must judge her under the most nearly normal conditions possible, not as a person trying to behave naturally while suffering from almost unbearable stress.

But to repeat, first impressions do count, and I will waste no time, for example, on an actress who enters my office wearing "shades" and showing some reluctance to taking them off. If her eyes show the results of a sleepless night, that is her misfortune. If I am not to be deprived of most of my basis for proper judgment, I must be able to see her eyes at all times. The eyes are probably the most important single feature of any actor's presence or personality (have you ever seen a dull-eyed movie star?), and unless I can see them as we talk I cannot properly judge whether or not they can bring life to a character on the screen.

I do have my prejudices, and one of them is sloppy dress. Sloppiness may be chic in your environment; it isn't in mine. An actress' manner of dressing gives me some sense of her consideration for others, as well as offering a healthy hint concerning her level of taste. Overdressing for the occasion is as bad as sloppiness; and though taste in clothing does not necessarily guarantee taste in character portrayal, more often than not it does help to make a decent impression.

The same, of course, can be said for make-up and hair styling. "Punk" hair-dos maybe "in" in your set. I find them distasteful. Something attractive but not too startling is unquestionably safer and probably better. Remember, at this point we are discussing impressions, not ability. You may have no opportunity to show your wares if my first impression discourages a favorable assessment of your personality.

As always, however, there is an exception. If some inside source (most probably your agent) has given you an accurate tip on the character up for grabs, by all means dress the part. If an accent is required, use it, but only if you are very, very good at accents. However, this can be a make-or-break situation, so be careful. If your information has been inaccurate and you dress as a street walker when the director is looking for a Bryn Mawr co-ed, you can blow the whole deal. So be quite sure of what you are doing, or play it safe and be yourself.

Given a positive first impression, I usually spend a few minutes in casual conversation about anything but the purpose of the interview. Some lessening of tension is the first order of business, and it gives me the opportunity to gather at least a slight impression of the actor's character. For it is that character I must deal with before we can arrive at a character on the screen, and some knowledge of his personality is needed before I can assume that there will be a good working relationship on the set.

Unless the actor has a super-clever agent, he is probably in the dark about the nature of the part for which he is being considered. When it is time to get down to business I will disclose the role I have in mind, its purpose and its character. If my impression is positive up to this point I will probably let him read (to himself) a scene from the script. But at this point I will never ask for a "cold" reading. Some actors are quite adept at sight readings, while others find them difficult, and ability to sight-read is not an accurate measure of acting talent. Montgomery Clift read like a rank illiterate, yet few would question the brilliance of his final characterizations.

The interview draws to a close, and if I consider the actor a promising candidate I will ask if he has any film he considers a good showcase for his ability. Film is always the easiest, and usually the best, source of such information, and if the answer is positive I will make arrangements to view it, using it as a basis for my final decision. If, on the other hand, the actor has no film or considers what he has to be inadequate or inappropriate, I ask him to prepare a scene for a live reading.

Some actors already have such scenes in their repertoire, usually something they have worked on in an acting class, something in which they feel secure. But such scenes, as a rule, bear no relationship to the character in question, and the performance may be too practiced, so they do not always serve the director's purpose. In my experience, it does no good, and it can work active harm, to play Ophelia when the character the director wants to see is a "hip" kid in the 1980s. That is why I usually ask the candidate to study a scene from my script as the best material for the test reading.

If the scene requires a second actor (and it usually does), I ask the actor to bring along the other reader. This might be the actor's coach (if he attends acting classes) or it might be the most suitable member of his circle of acting friends.

In any case, no sensible director ever takes an active part in such a reading. One cannot be a competent participant and an honest observer at the same time, and here objective observation is all important.

At such a reading I look for a number of things: How well has the actor learned his lines in the time available? Does he know them well enough to be able to be "with" his acting partner as he reads? Does he listen to him? Does he look directly at him to make his points? Can he "throw away" a casual line and still maintain his vitality? Does he have vitality? Are his reactions spontaneous or contrived? If the scene calls for laughter, does he laugh easily and well? If it calls for tears, can he manufacture his own? If the scene demands anger, does he maintain control of his voice? Can I see the "acting wheels" turning in his brain?

I do not expect perfection in any of these areas, but if the actor can get a B+ across most of the board he will probably get the job. Then the real work starts, for that series of questions relates to a good deal of what acting for the screen is all about. In the succeeding chapters we discuss them in detail.

*   *   *

The actress speaks:

When called for an interview, the first thing I do is ask my agent, or whoever, "What's the part, and what's the story like?" I will be given either very little or quite a bit of information. It's whatever he knows. It could be only, "They want a prostitute"; but on the other hand, he might say, "They need a darling girl to play opposite John Travolta." And just hope *he says,*

"They're looking for someone different." That's what you must keep in mind. With all the copying done today, too many people look alike, sound alike, and act alike. Be an individual. Believe me, it is someone different, with something new to flash, who will get the part.

If you're given a clue as to the kind of part you're going for, set that deep in your mind and start preparing to be just that. Dress for it, make up (or down) for it, and actually take the character apart and build your own background for her. If you're fortunate enough to have been told what the whole story is about, that makes it easier. You know then how and why your character "is there," and what happens to her.

At this point, let me say that rarely is an actor called for a part that doesn't suit. The casting office and/or the director have seen photos or perhaps your work, and what they have seen fits what they have in mind. Above all, don't ever go after a part you don't feel is right for you. But if you sincerely want it, and you're given the opportunity to show what you can do—go get it!

From the moment you are called you think of nothing else. You don't go out, you picture yourself as the character, and you live with it as much as you can until the actual interview. Then you walk into the director's office with as much self-assurance as you can muster.

You are introduced by the secretary, and you will usually find several people in the room; perhaps the producer, the writer, and sometimes a dialogue director to read lines with you. A first-class director never reads with you—he needs to watch every move you make, every expression, every reaction. He must watch you as you hear the dialogue being spoken as though you've never seen or heard it before. Often, it is what's in between the lines that proves to be most important.

The director is cordial and tries to make you feel at ease with a little small talk. Try your best to make him think you are at ease so you can get on with it.

The moment comes for the reading. If you have been sent the script, know it. Have it memorized. Know all the lines—his and hers and yours. Know the scene so perfectly that it seems a part of your life that you are allowing them to look in on. If you have been handed the scene in the outer office just a half-hour before, do your best to learn it well enough to look up from the pages as often as possible, especially at crucial points, to show that you have a clear understanding and feel for the character.

When the reading is over, you are never sure whether they liked it or not. Even if you feel you have made a good presentation—even if the director says, "Very good!"—don't believe him. You are rarely told, "The part is yours," right there on the spot.

You thank them all, with charm and poise, and if you can remember their names (especially the director's) it's a point in your favor to say goodbye to each one personally.

As you close the door behind you, your hands trembling unnoticeably, you say goodbye cheerily to the secretary, take a quick count and account of the waiting actresses (if there are any), and out you go.

You can't think of anything else. You aren't hungry. You call your agent as soon as you get home to report your views on how it went. If you don't hear something before bedtime you try to eat a little and you try, unsuccessfully, to sleep. You imagine many things . . . your hair was wrong . . . you should have stood instead of sat . . . they didn't like you. Then you question it all. Are you right for the part? Is there someone better? You toss and turn and finally drop off just before you must get up. Every actor has a full day. As soon as you know your agent is in the office you call to let him know where you'll be throughout the day.

You barely make it through the aerobics class, and stumble to the health bar for a snack. If you have an answering service you check that out. Nothing. You go for your voice lesson and have never felt less like singing; but you sing. The show must go on, and all that. After all, if you don't get this part there will be another one to audition for, and you must work to be at your best. But here's the secret. If you're going to get the part, you really feel it, deep down. Of course, this is where some of the greatest disappointments occur. A person knows she's done a good job, and feels she's clinched the part. But what has happened during that endless time between the interview and the decision? It may have ended with the part being given to a better-known name, or to someone whose appearance fits more readily

with the rest of the cast, or—God forbid, for this is hard to take—
to the girlfriend of one of the executives.

You're home at last, still able to function, but barely. You
make yourself a cup of herb tea, and the phone rings.

You've got the part!

You thought you were excited before, but now all hell breaks
loose! You scream with delight—the dog howls with you. You're
on the phone to all your friends, and finally to your mother.

The agent has told you the script would be sent over by special
messenger, so you don't dare go out. Pizza is delivered. The script
hasn't arrived and it's bedtime. You call your agent. He calls
you a pest, but you know he loves you. You've just made him
a few bucks. He promises to check with the studio tomorrow.

The doorbell rings, and it's the script. "Hello, script! Oh, you
marvelous thing, you!" You devour it. Up all night. Great. Great.
Even though you're not the lead, you can make this part important. You turn off the phone and sleep late the next morning.

As you plug in the phone, it rings. Your agent is mad. He's
been trying to reach you to tell you the script has been sent and
that you are to report to the studio for wardrobe fittings in one
hour.

You make it, of course. You find that the director has already
okayed suggestions made by the wardrobe designer for the character you are playing. All she (or he) has to do is choose a color
that suits you, one that will blend with colors worn by other
actors you will be playing scenes with. Wardrobe departments
do a good job preparing far ahead of time for the whole film. By
the time shooting starts you know what you'll be wearing in
every scene.

If required at this time, you may be sent to the makeup and
hairdressing department. The makeup man (or lady) likes to see,
well ahead of time, the people who are to play key characters.
He has read the script, knows the characters and the scenes, and
has in mind what they should look like. Hair styles are suggested
and agreed upon between you and the department heads, subject, of course, to the director's approval.

You go home after a very full and exciting day, chat with your
friends on the phone, assure your mom that everything is perfect,
play with the dog, do a few (neglected) exercises. Then you pick
up the script and get serious.

Your call is to be on the set, ready to shoot, at 9:00 AM, Monday. This means a 7 o'clock makeup call, and that means getting up at 6:00. You will not go out all weekend. You will study the scene (or scenes) to be played on Monday. You will eat carefully and well, and you will be sure to get enough sleep. Your eyes must be clear and your mind must be alert.

During the weekend you will imagine how things will go. Reading the script, you can picture the set in your mind, even see yourself moving around in it. Once the film is under way you can usually count on visiting the other sets you will be working on. This helps in the preparation of the scenes involved. As you lie in bed and envision Monday's scene, you wonder if the director is seeing it as you are. What is he like? What do you know about him? What does he know about you? Have you heard that he is difficult? No. You don't really know anything. But you've had enough experience to know that he is boss. However, you mustn't be afraid to try things, even if they're not written in the script—especially if they're not written in the script. You've made notes on ideas to ask him about.

You wonder what the other actors will be like. You pride yourself on being able to work with all sorts of people, so you can certainly handle other actors. Your thoughts return to the director, and you call your agent to see if you can find out more about him. Your agent calls you a pest, but he fills you in on whatever he knows about the director and his way of working. You feel better. Above all, you want what the director wants. You crawl again into the character you are becoming, and you build her history. Where was she born? What were her parents like? What was her childhood like? What are her favorite foods? Colors? Does she like animals, or is she frightened of cats? Judging by her relationships with others in the script you will know how to play her. Now you wonder why the director chose you. Because you are perfect for the part. Knowing this, you are finally able to sleep.

The alarm goes off. It's 6 o'clock, and you're up like a shot. A tablespoon of honey and a glass of hot lemon water, steam the face with hot water, oil on the face, then cold water to close the pores. Into a pair of jeans and a top, and you're off. Total happiness. You rehearse your lines all the way to the studio.

Hollywood is a unique and wondrous place. As you pass other

cars on the road, three out of four of the drivers will appear to be talking to themselves. Actually, they are rehearsing their lines while they are on their way to cut a record, do a commercial, or play a part in a film. It's a trick we have out here; driving unconsciously so that we can concentrate on something else.

You are on time for your makeup call. The makeup department of a studio is one of my favorite spots. It is warm and exciting, and it's fun. There's always coffee and doughnuts or danish. The first day is made easy by this wonderful group of experts. The studios hire only the best in this field, and they're well seasoned, with mounds of experience. Each one is quick to figure you out. They know you instantly. Some will try you with little jokes and one-liners, and you watch them banter with each other. When you are alone with one, he (or she) will quickly tell you about all of the others. By the time your hair has been shampooed and styled and your makeup is finished, you feel you've known them all for ages.

Along the line here, between 7:00 and 9:00, one of the assistant directors will be checking to see where you are, to be certain that you and all the other actors will be on the set on time.

To be "on time" is your most important assignment in the routine end of the business. Every minute counts when shooting a film. Each minute literally costs thousands of dollars. The production department works hard to set up a schedule that will be most economically efficient for all concerned. When you are hired, the company expects you to be where you are told to be at exactly the time you are told to be there. There are no excuses and no mistakes.

If your part in the film is important enough, you will be assigned a dressing room on the lot as well as a portable dressing room on the set. If you are this lucky, on the first day of production your wardrobe lady will meet you in the makeup department, take you to your dressing room, and help you into your costume. Your dressing room is your sanctuary and should be treated with reverence. Here you can rest, study, and think, and be completely alone. And an actress never invites a man into her lot dressing room. She is watched, and this is a no-no. As silly as it may sound to many of you, I hope you will remember it and consider it carefully. The film business is a serious business, and you do not want to get a reputation for *playing around at work. Make dates for off the lot, and not during working hours.*

After the wardrobe lady has checked your clothes, you touch up your makeup and your hair, then glance at your first scene again. You are ready. You head for the set.

Serious discussions of character take place during the first read-ing, which usually precedes the scene to be shot. Here Dmytryk talks about a script with Gregory Peck and Diane Baker for **Mirage.**

2

The Reading

Few scripts are so profound that an intelligent actor will find it difficult to understand the background, intent, or characterizations involved. That, of course, is an exaggeration. No script is that profound. One that is will attract a small audience indeed. It makes no sense to assume that the script for a film made to appeal to an average audience, which means it must be understood by that audience, is so abstruse as to be beyond the grasp of the average actor.

Here let me say that I have never met a good actor who was unintelligent. On the contrary, the great majority of competent actors range the scale from quite to very bright. It is only the occasional writer's or director's ego, smarting at the sight of the public attention, even adulation, heaped on performers, that leads him to pretend that he possesses an esoteric knowledge of the script's characters and content denied to the actors. The director who is sometimes quoted as saying, "Actors are puppets," is probably pulling the interviewer's leg. In any case, his next film will belie his words by exhibiting the most creative cast he can buy.

There may be some casual exchange of information between actor and director during an office visit to discuss wardrobe, makeup, and the like, but understanding of character and content is usually taken for granted. Any discussion of them, if it takes place at all, is usually left to the first rehearsal, and then it will probably concern itself with further developments and nuances rather than with basic understanding. That understanding has been there from the first reading of the script. If not, if the actors express some confusion about the screenplay and its inhabitants, it is not the artists but the script that needs overhauling.

No two directors work exactly alike, but in my experience, the first serious discussion of conception and realization of character takes place during the readings, which usually precede the first rehearsals of the first scenes to be shot. Many directors set this up for the first day of filming. Whenever possible, I prefer to arrange such a rehearsal for the day preceding the start of actual production. At this time, neither the cast, the crew, nor I are under any pressure. The butterflies have not yet started to flutter or, if they have, they do so feebly; bodies are relaxed and minds are clear and more willing to range abroad. An atmosphere of exploration can now be established that will last throughout the greater part of the schedule. In keeping with this more relaxed atmosphere, I ask my actors to read and rehearse in a casual manner, to make no effort to go all out emotionally this early in the proceedings. When the actors *do* go all out emotionally, I want it on film.

Readings come first. Before the camera is brought near the set or a single light is lit, everyone must know how the scene is to go. (It will not necessarily *play* as well as it reads.) At this stage the director has a good idea of how the scene is to be staged, of how it should be played, but his early conceptions must not blind him to new, possibly superior, avenues that may open up when the actors are allowed to offer their contributions.

The first sequence to be shot is the subject of the reading. That sequence may be short or scheduled for three or more days of filming. The reading should cover the entire sequence, regardless of its length.

A reading is the time for testing, for listening, for molding, and for editing. The reading, which is not really a reading, since most of the cast know their lines, allows the director to hear the actors and the actors to hear each other for the first time. It is a fresh, occasionally a startling experience. Even though the performances are not full bore, the manner of playing and the range of vitality contained in the scene quickly become apparent. A line of dialogue spoken by an actor may differ considerably from the other actors' conceptualization of that line. That, in turn, may result in an alteration in the reactions, both physical and vocal, of one or more of the other members of the cast.

One of the most important things for an actor to understand is that acting is rarely a solo performance. Other actors are involved, and if a scene is to be played at its best, their concepts and their manners of execution inevitably affect his—as they should. A truly responsible and responsive actor will find that his own concepts and the understanding of his character and dialogue are broadened by the contact and interplay with the creative ideas of the other actors in the scene.

Regardless of the ideas an actor may have conceived in preparation for this moment, during the first reading he should closely follow the script. Many changes, or none, may eventually be made in the scene, but at this point it is unreasonable to assume that changes are inevitable or necessary. It is possible that the writer has created a gem. It is now the actor's duty to do it justice. If changes are to be made, it is almost always the director who leads the way.

This must be mentioned here because scripts can be freely rewritten, and they occasionally are, not always to the benefit of the film. Once in a great while an actor may propose changes solely to establish himself as a presence, not because he truly finds shortcomings in the script. Honest suggestions will be considered by most directors (although, as a rule, few find their way to the screen) but they should be based on an intelligent analysis of the character, the scene, and the effect the changes may have on the other characters in it, rather than on a desire to bolster one's own ego, or one's part.

As the readings progress and the actors become more comfortable with the scene and with each other, suggestions can be made without arousing any shock, and only a little suspicion. An actor may have found that a certain kind of shrug says, "I don't care," or "I don't know," far more effectively than does the spoken line. He should try it. If it fits, and the responding actors react naturally to the character and not just to the line, they will probably accept the meaning of the shrug without realizing that the line itself has been omitted. The director will probably note it with silent approval; he may even have had something of the sort in mind, and doesn't resent being beaten to the punch. He will also realize that the actor's sense of security has reached a solid level—the actor is now ready to offer, and to accept, changes.

The readings may reveal further redundancies, not only in those instances where actions or attitudes can replace lines, but more commonly on lines that are verbose. Rarely is there need at this stage for additional information through dialogue; deletion is usually the order of the day.

There is an important, though often ignored, facet in this area of acting. A silent action such as the shrug or a subtle change in attitude allows, sometimes forces, the viewer to involve himself in the scene (and the film) by asking him to furnish his own "lyrics." The actor shrugs, and the viewer thinks, "Aha, he doesn't care." He is directly engaged. If the line is spoken, he simply sits back and listens, he has no incentive to do more. But the goal of a well-made film or a well-turned performance is to weave the viewer into the fabric of the film, to make him a participant in the action. The more effectively an actor can do this the more highly he will be regarded. Once upon a time actors counted their lines and evaluated their worth by their number. But Jane Wyman won an Academy Award for playing a mute, and Douglas Fairbanks, Sr. was wont to say, "Give most of the words to the other actors—just let me have the toppers."

The readings will also reveal the scene's viability or lack of it. A scene may read well but refuse to come to life when played. This is not an infrequent occurrence. The perceptive director will immediately start looking for the fault and the cure. Here is where an actor's instinct can be valuable. Occasionally the entire scene is sick; more often it is a dishonest line or two, an unbelievable bit of characterization, or the indication of an inappropriate mood. In most of these cases a correction can be found that does not require radical surgery, but once in a great while the whole scene must be scrapped.

In order to survive the rocking of the boat, the actor must be adaptable. He must remain unthreatened, even though his lines, and sometimes his concepts, are changed; "evolved" is a more positive word. There can be trouble in paradise, of course, if the actor is not convinced that such changes are an improvement on his original conception or the original scene. Fortunately, however, conflicts in this area are few.

To be on solid ground during these proceedings, the actor should have done as much homework as time has allowed. A contemporary character is easy to accommodate, but in stories dealing with other times and other places, books are usually the best source of information. They should be studied and absorbed until the pertinent knowledge has become second nature. For contemporary situations and characters that may be somewhat removed from the familiar, direct contact and communication is often possible. An actress may be playing an only daughter, but she, herself, comes from a large family. She should find an only daughter (she probably already knows more than one) and question her, grill her if necessary. She won't learn the whole story, but she will get a feel. Playing a woman cop? Talk to one. If possible, accompany her on her rounds. It can be done.

In extreme cases, prepare to sacrifice a good deal of time and a fat slice of your peace of mind. In *The Snake Pit*, Olivia DeHaviland played a woman forced to spend time in a mental institution. She committed herself to one for, I believe, a period of two weeks. Under the best of circumstances it must have been a heart- and mind-wrenching experience, but it resulted in an Oscar-winning performance. A more squeamish actress could hardly have done as well.

Readings are usually not too difficult or too long. Sometimes there is little or nothing to be improved. But when one does expose a problem, a successful solution will eliminate most of the questionable elements of the scene. It is now set, but it still remains to be fully realized. The next step in the procedure is rehearsal.

* * *

The actress speaks:

Everyone loves the movies, and almost everyone who comes to Hollywood wants to visit a "movie studio." That means they hope to set foot on a real sound stage and get a glimpse of what film making is all about.

The sound stage is huge. It must accommodate several sets with walls of normal height while leaving plenty of space aloft for the enormous lights that are needed. Above the imaginary walls are scaffolds upon which electricians walk while tending their lights. Sometimes there is need for a crane on which the camera moves about. The stage is usually square, with doors on at least two sides, often three. Huge doors that roll open are for the big items. Beside each of these is a normal, warehouse-type door, but it is double. The first door allows you in from the studio street, but at the top of the second door is a light, and if that light is glowing red it signifies that the company inside is shooting, and not a sound can be made. You must wait until the light goes off before entering through the second door. The entire stage is padded, soundproofed. Unless the film is a comedy, a musical, or a musical comedy, most stages are very, very quiet. And very dark.

I walked into Stage 6 and found it very quiet and very dark. Carefully stepping over large cables, I made my way to one side. As my eyes adjusted, I saw light up ahead and heard voices. A laugh lightened my step. I came upon the set, not yet lit, and I noticed the director and some of the crew chatting and having coffee. The assistant director came to me and offered to show me to my set dressing room. The director immediately spoke my name and said pleasantly, "Don't get too comfortable, we're going to have a reading as soon as everyone's here."

Trying to be very businesslike, I went into my portable dressing room and placed a few things on the makeup table, calling it "mine." It's important to have a place of your own to withdraw to while in the middle of another world. That makeup table, with all the lights surrounding it, makes you feel like a star, but you quickly remind yourself that you're not—not yet. I picked up my script and returned to the set. The other actors were there.

The director was jovial and spoke of some humorous article in the morning's paper, which led the leading man into a story of his own. He was a name actor, so I had seen his work, but I was not acquainted with him. This gave me the opportunity to look him over, to laugh at his joke, to make eye-to-eye contact and let him know I was friendly. The other actress seemed composed. I wondered what she was composed of. Beauty, for sure. But there was no jealousy here. Far from it. I wanted to appear professional, so I was hanging back until I was on.

The director took charge, told us where to sit and took his place in his own chair, which had been carefully placed where he could easily watch us. The leading lady opened her script to the scene. I did the same. The leading man said he didn't have his script with him, could he use someone else's? One was quickly handed to him. (Was he going to be a problem?) We all knew our lines, but the scripts are always kept at hand in case there are any changes made for later study. The crew stood quietly by, and the director said, "Okay, let's have a listen."

The leading man started the scene, and I thought he was terrific. The other actress had a line, and she was okay. She was beautiful. My lines were coming up. I hadn't realized I was nervous, and I was late in speaking. I knew it, but the director didn't say a word. He let the scene finish with no interruptions.

"Now," he said, "I have just a few suggestions." I knew it. I bit my lip. "Since each of you knows the entire story," he continued, "you know what has happened prior to this scene, and you know what follows. Let's see if we can't get more comfortable with the characters, get them to know each other."

He then cut out a few pauses that had been written in for the leading lady and suggested that she interrupt the leading man at one point, tightening the scene. And, of course, he wanted me on my toes—no dead air, shall we say? He spoke to us softly and kindly, but we were well aware of the importance behind what he was saying. He wanted something special from each of us.

An on-the-set reading can be different with each director. I had done a small part in a less important film not long before, and only enough time was spent on the reading to show that we knew our lines, after which we went quickly into the set for a rehearsal. Within half an hour we had our first set-up "in the can." (For those of you who don't know this expression, it means completed, in the tin, since rolls of finished film are placed in a flat, round tin can.) Naturally, this technique does not turn out the quality one might desire, but time is money, and sometimes there just isn't enough time or money for a director to get exactly what he wants on film. So he does the best he can. He expects the actors to know their lines perfectly and, more often than not, to stick to the script as it's written.

For live TV, the readings are of prime importance. I was once contracted for two weeks to do a one-hour live show, and was called in every day. The whole cast sat around a large table and read the whole script over and over. It was much like theater work, except that we could make changes. The director was good in his field, but the pressure of this job made him irritable and unsure of himself. By the time we were ready to shoot, live, in front of an audience, even Agnes Moorehead had vowed never to do live TV again. And she didn't. This is the most difficult on-camera acting, because you can't be natural while worrying about tripping over cables as you change costume on the run, hoping to walk calmly through a doorway. Though many jokes are made after it's over, it is deadly. But you can see why the readings are so important.

Back to the present situation; the director called for another reading. We were much more relaxed and the timing was improved. He did break in here and there until we were close to what he wanted. He told us not to give our total emotion, to save it for the camera, so I was anxious to get going.

The scene we were preparing to shoot would come in the middle of the film, so my character was not only familiar with the other two, she had had a fight with the leading lady, gone on the make for the leading man, been rejected by him, and had lied to her father (a local gentleman of power) to get the leading man in trouble.

The director called for the cameraman, and told us we would now move into the set for a rehearsal. Everyone listens when the director talks, and tries to anticipate his plans. All of a sudden the set was lit by several large lights and it was daytime in a ranch house somewhere in the West.

In this scene from Metro-Goldwyn-Meyer's humorous tale of teen-age autograph seekers, The Youngest Profession, *pert Jean Porter is surrounded by a cast that includes Edward Arnold, Marta Linden, and Agnes Moorehead.*

3

The Rehearsal

The scene has been analyzed, the lines set, and the characters developed and integrated, but there is more to be considered. How and where do the scene's participants move? Or do they? Most scenes do of course, contain movement, but no law makes movement mandatory. Physical movement, though often advantageous, is not a given for all scenes.

Today, many students and young filmmakers appear to believe that physical, mechanical (i.e., movement of the camera), or editorial (cutting) movement is necessary to keep a scene interesting. This is a misconception, and is valid only as an ameliorative technique in the event that a scene is badly written or inadequately realized. The movement that should concern the filmmaker is that which takes place in the viewer's mind, and the actors play a most important part in the process that makes such movement possible. A scene can be completely effective without the staging of a single move if that scene is well written, well played, and of real consequence.

A scene in one of Orson Welles's films showed several people discussing, at great length, an important family problem. They sat in a loose group, more or less immobile, for several minutes, yet the scene remained vital, moving, and alive. On more than one occasion I have allowed a scene in which the actors were relatively quiescent to run, uncut, for nearly ten minutes because I felt that any arbitrary move or cut would have been simply gilding the lily and just as artificial.

It is still true, however, that most scenes contain physical movement, movement whose purpose is to disclose "business," to reveal or conceal emotion, or to express physical nervousness or inner tension. For example, a character may walk over to a desk to pick up a relevant paper; or he may turn away from the other participants in the scene and walk a few steps in order to hide an emotion or a tell-tale reaction, or simply to gather his thoughts before turning back to continue the conversation. He may stand up or walk to relieve some tension building up in his mind or body or, on an exterior location, talk to a companion while walking toward his parked car or the entrance to his apartment.

Movement is also used to accentuate dramatic timing. A pause, while seated, may appear to be simply a stall, but the same pause, or even a longer break in the conversation, can project a great deal more meaning if the actor is allowed to express the unuttered conflict or change in attitude through movement. Just as a vital reaction can be heightened if the reactor is looking away at the moment of thought impact, and is forced to turn sharply toward the person speaking,* so more extensive moves can be used to accentuate those transitions which are the life blood of every well-written and well-realized scene.

It is important for the actor to understand that any such movement should be made for a reason and made decisively. Nothing can deflate a scene as quickly as a weak, tentative move. If one player walks away from another in order to withdraw, say, from an embarrassment, a confrontation, or a verbal challenge, that move must be made purposefully. At such a moment, sauntering will completely undercut the desired effect. As a matter of fact, it is hard to conceive of a situation in which a casual or lethargic move is useful, except when such a move has a specific dramatic purpose. In short, actors must consider their moves as thoroughly as they do their lines, and then proceed to incorporate them skillfully into their performances.

(A scene stands out vividly in my mind: I am staging a shot for *Raintree County* in which Monty Clift enters a bedroom where his wife, Elizabeth Taylor, pregnant, out of sorts, and restless, lies uncomfortably in bed. As he enters the room Clift's left

---

*This acting trick, however, must be used sparingly, for obvious reasons.

hand swings the door shut behind him, but his right hand, also behind him, catches it before it can slam shut. Taking a short step backward, he closes the door softly. Only then does he move toward the bed and his wife.

After the rehearsal, while the cameraman was lighting the set, Clift spent at least twenty minutes in practice. He would walk through the door, swing it behind him, catch it in motion, then softly close it, all without any apparent attention to the action. He wanted to make it look as though he had been through *that* door, in *his* bedroom, in *his* home, a thousand times, and that the whole procedure was strictly second nature, performed without the slightest conscious thought. And that's exactly how it looked when we finally filmed the scene.)

The rehearsal that follows the reading takes all these aspects of movement into consideration. Indeed, that is its prime purpose. The movement rehearsal, or staging, is always initiated by the director. Most probably, he already has his basic set-ups (camera positions) in mind, and his staging, at least in the early rehearsals, will be determined by such plans. However, the creative director will always leave the door open for further development of concept and movement as the rehearsals progress. As a rule, his concept will hold and few if any changes will be called for; but as the actors work their way into the scene and begin to feel at home with it in all of its aspects, opportunities to improve the flow or the effectiveness of the scene may occasionally arise. An actor's suggestion in this regard will rarely be rejected out of hand.

However, the actor should always be aware of an important consideration. Some suggestions may be impractical because they do not suit the director's filming and cutting concepts. A movement may be too broad, for instance, to be easily accommodated by the most effective set-ups, or it may be conceived without due regard to the movements and/or positions of the scene's other actors. Many directors will treat such suggestions summarily, dismissing them quickly, with or without explanation. On the other hand, only an insecure director would refuse to incorporate into his scheme of things a suggestion bringing improvement to the scene's content or effectiveness. In any event, the making of such a suggestion is worth the risk. Even one success in twenty attempts can serve to sweeten the pot.

Once the rehearsal has fixed movement and position, and the actors have begun to find themselves comfortable with the scene and with each other, the rest of the crew takes over. While the film machinery is moved into place and the cameraman starts to light the set and the stand-ins, the actors retire to their dressing rooms and their separate activities, whether they be rehearsing lines, dressing for the scene, or freshening makeup. At this time, any lingering doubts or uncertainties should be discussed with the director, because the next step is the real thing. The culmination of all the preparation, the studying, the reading, and the rehearsal, will now be fixed on film and tape or, as they say on the set, "recorded for posterity."

*   *   *

The actress speaks:

The set was a large living room, with an entryway and staircase in the background. Two walls were movable to accommodate camera placement. The scene called for my character to come down the stairs, see the other two talking in the living room, and go to them. Their conversation is interrupted by my entrance.

My tendency is to move too fast. I had been told that more than once before on film jobs, so I planned to be more careful this time. But the young girl I was playing was bouncy, bright, and, because of her youth, much too sure of herself.

While the crew watched, the director called for a rehearsal. The cameraman stood with the director. The other two actors and I had exchanged a few words and walked around the set, touching the furniture, getting acquainted with the props.

This was my home. The leading lady was my sister and the leading man had been her beau. He had gone away to college and was back in town before taking a job somewhere up north. While he was away studying, big sister had become involved with a new man around town and little sister (that's me!) had grown up. (You think you know the whole story already, don't you?)

I went to the top of the staircase, getting the feel of the stairs that I must treat as though I had been up and down them daily for eighteen years. I counted them, measured their width in comparison with my feet. In drama school I had learned a dozen ways to climb stairs and float, or clamber, down. This girl should be light on her feet but, most of all, completely unaware of the movement.

"All right, let's go," the director said. He had placed the two stars where he wanted them to stand and gave me an idea of where I should end up. "Just a run-through," he said.

I ran to the top of the stairs, then reminded myself to stop running. Slow down! This is what I had to keep in mind.

"Action!" the director said, and I was off. I scooted down the stairs, neatly nonchalant, paused near the bottom as I spotted the two people in the living room standing close to each other, talking quietly. Then I moved toward them until I reached the point at which I had been told to stop.

The leading man—let's call him Ben—had his back to the stairway and had not seen me. My sister's reaction to my entry was to reach out and touch him to stop his talking, and her look to me drew his attention in my direction. This part of the scene was mine.

Here is a very important thing to be aware of and to remember. You find yourself realizing how important the scene is to the story, and how important your part is to the scene. If the scene is totally concerned with the information you are giving the viewer through dialogue and/or action, you can become awfully cocky. You are certain that you can't be cut out and that you can't be cut away from, either. The scene is yours. Watch out! This is the disease called Star Syndrome. Whether you are the star or not. All of a sudden a kind of euphoria sets in, and you can do no wrong. You have all kinds of ideas that are perfect.

Now is the time for all good men to come to the aid of this person—she is in trouble. Now is the time you must listen carefully to the director and believe what you hear. Like a pilot, you'd better believe the instruments.

This is not meant to curb your enthusiasm or squelch your desire to incorporate some innovative ideas that have come to your mind, but if you're not careful at this point, you can annihilate your relationship with the director and the other actors. When you have everything, be generous.

The director gently moved me to one side and spoke quietly. I had come down the stairs too fast and moved forward too

*quickly, not giving anyone else time to do anything. I apologized,
and told him I would move more slowly. I went back up the
stairs, he called "Action" again, and I pulled in the reins. It even
felt better. I had thought the previous rehearsal was okay, but
when it's right, you know it. I came down the stairs lightly,
paused at the sight of the two, and sauntered over to them. The
timing was right for the other actors, giving them time to react.*

*My sister had the first line as I reached them, so it was sug-
gested by the director that I pass her and plop down on the
couch. Her eyes followed me as she spoke, which put her on
camera. Now all three of us were in good camera view.*

*She wasted no time at all in chastising me for what I had
done. As the rehearsals continued, I did a good job of listening.
Then I had my turn. By this time I was on my feet, walking
slowly around them. Suddenly I stopped for the big clincher line.
I looked directly into my sister's eyes, spoke quietly, and soon
the tears started to roll down my cheeks. Up to this point everyone in the audience found my character a naughty little smart-
alec, and would have liked to see her done in. Now they had to
weep for the poor darling.*

This is what it's all about.

*One must be technically skilled enough to fake any mood,
yet make it believable. You must believe it.*

*Movement was as much a part of the scene as the dialogue.
As we rehearsed, it all came together. With the director's guid-
ance, the movements became so natural that a move would bring
forth a line, or stop someone in the middle of a sentence. By the
time we were ready to shoot the first set-up, we knew how the
whole sequence would go and we were comfortable with each
other.*

*After being told to freshen our makeup and to get ready to
shoot, the director came up beside me and walked with me
toward my dressing room.*

*"You're really doing a good job," he said, "but I told you to
hold back the emotion—the tears—during the rehearsal. I don't
want you all cried out."*

"Oh, that's all right. I can't help it," I answered.

*"Those were real tears. How come you can cry so easily?" he
asked.*

"Hey. In this world, the way it is, it's holding back the tears

that's difficult. When given an open invitation to cry, that's easy."

It just so happened that my part was well written, and I understood the inside workings of this character from having known people like her. Getting to know and understand people in every walk of life, all situations, is the key. Of course, it can be heartbreaking. And you will cry.

Actors and actresses must learn to limit their field of attention and block out the presence of the camera, the director, and the crew. Edward Dmytryk directs Guy Madison and Jean Porter in a scene from Till the End of Time.

4

Where Did Everyone Go?

The set is lit. Last-minute rehearsals for sound and camera have been held. Lighting retouches have been completed. The time for shooting has arrived. What does the director look for in the playing of a scene?

First of all, are the actors working with each other or are they too aware of external distractions? The necessity to concentrate on the scene on the one hand, and awareness of people and objects on the stage surrounding the immediate set on the other, confront the actor with contradictory apprehensions.

Two technical, nonacting requirements are ever present, and they can be counterproductive. First is the need to "hit the marks" accurately—to stay within the range of the key lights. The director sets up his camera for the positions and movements that will most effectively capture the players' reactions and the mood of the scene. In turn, the cameraman sets his lights for those positions, and movement at those positions may be narrowly restricted. So the actors must hit their marks with some accuracy if the lighting and the resulting recorded images are to be satisfactory. Yet they must never reveal, by attitude, reaction, or conscious bodily adjustment, that they are searching for their marks or reaching them.

Concentrating more on the marks than on the substance of the scene produces a mechanical performance. An actor cannot possibly involve himself completely in the dramatic give-and-

31

take of a scene while worrying about his position relative to the camera and his key light.

Experienced actors have learned to take these requirements in stride. Like heat-seeking missiles, they "feel" a key light instinctively, and if they are in it they are most probably on their marks. Beyond that, they can reduce the problem by relating their moves to other actors or to objects on the set—a table, a chair or sofa, or some other piece of set dressing that may be at hand.

Of course, a considerate director can make it somewhat easier for the actor by asking the cameraman to light more broadly (though well short of "flat" lighting), thus giving the player some leeway in his moves. Only in close shots is exact positioning of prime importance, and most such set-ups call for little movement from the actor.

This is one of the more difficult adjustments a screen actor must make, but once he has learned to accommodate it instinctively, he can become freely and completely involved in the scene itself—well, almost.

The second necessary adjustment may be even more difficult. The actor must learn to limit his field of attention. He must black out the presence of the camera, the director, and the crew. This is made somewhat easier for him by an obligatory convention; off-the-set lights are usually extinguished, leaving everything except the set in darkness. Crew members retire to the back of the stage or behind the camera. The actors' "eye-lines," those directions in which they look during any part of the scene, are kept free of people or objects that might attract or distract the actors' attention. The director places himself close to the camera or even under it. This enables him to see the scene from the camera's point of view and serves to diminish his visibility.

All this is done to facilitate the actor's effort to "live" with his collaborators in the scene. He must listen to them, react to them, and speak to them, not for the camera, the director, or the crew. For the good screen actor there is no audience, only fellow beings involved in a happening of substance. It is the only way a scene can be made to come alive and include the viewer as a participant rather than as an on-looker.

Perhaps the best way for the actor to cut off the distractions of the real world is to listen to the people in his world of make-believe. Concentration on listening serves to tune out distractions, both audible and visual. Anyone who has held a quiet conversation in the midst of a babbling crowd can testify to that. So, the harder the actor listens the more effectively he is able to disregard the disturbances inherent in shooting on the set.

Of course, one must listen to the character, not the player, and rapt attention should not slop over into the area of self-hypnosis. During the shooting of *One-eyed Jacks*, an on-camera actor was listening to off-camera Marlon Brando delivering his off-stage lines. The actor's cue came—and went. He stood there spellbound and speechless.

"Cut!" yelled actor-director Brando, as he advanced on the actor. "Where, in God's name, *were* you?" he asked.

"Mar," replied the actor, "you were so wonderful, so over-powering, I was lost in admiration."

By that time the light was getting yellow, and Brando called it a day.

Stopping short of idol worship (or clever alibi), the most important skill an actor must develop is the ability to listen, which is not exactly a universal aptitude. Yet listening, really listening, not just pretending to, is the necessary prerequisite for nearly every other facet of screen acting; most of the actor's other skills—reacting, speaking dialogue, even movement—are inspired by what he hears.

The greatest compliment one actor can pay another is to say, "He gives me something!" What he appreciates is that his fellow player is heeding his words and observing his behavior; that he is, quite literally, giving him attention. And in keeping with the well-known biblical prescription, the giver derives more benefit from his gift than does the receiver.

The camera is a powerful telescope; just try to estimate the relative size of a normal close-up on a wide screen. If the actor is concentrating on his next line instead of listening to the speaker, it can be easily seen, especially in a close-up, but also, to somewhat less effect, in a medium shot as well. And by far the greater part of the average film consists of medium shots and close-ups. Only in the occasional long shot will the absence of listening escape the viewer's attention, and even then he may react subconsciously to the lack of a proper listening attitude.

Keen observation is a necessary concomitant of sharp listening. The good actor concerns himself not only with the proper delivery of a line of dialogue, but also with the physical manifestations that accompany it. In fuller shots these may include relatively broad gestures and body moves, but in large close-ups, where such gestures and moves are discouraged, there are still tiny displays of facial movements that commonly accompany speech. (A "frozen" face becomes an object of humor or of pity.) Such movements, whether they be broad or delicate, are an essential part of communication, both in real life and on the screen. They serve to underscore the meaning of the spoken words—or to belie them— but always they are unavoidable reinforcements. They supply nuances and almost always serve to round out the total message delivered in any line of dialogue.

With all this in mind, the actor must watch his fellow players intently (unless, of course, inattention or avoidance of visual contact is the point of the scene) and listen intently. When he does so his responses, both in reaction and in dialogue, will be generated by what he receives from the speaker, not just what he remembers of the script, and it will be much easier for him to make those responses appear spontaneous rather than arbitrary. At best, they *will* be spontaneous, and real-life spontaneity is the goal of every well-played scene.*

Here I am reminded that a third semitechnical adjustment is required in the search for spontaneity. It concerns the repetition of a scene or, more properly, a "take," while shooting. A few actors (Spencer Tracy, Humphrey Bogart, and Monty Clift come immediately to mind) have rarely needed more than one take to register their optimum performances. Obviously, they had a minimum amount of trouble in achieving spontaneity. Most actors, however, need several tries at reaching "perfection" (a few will climb to forty, fifty, or more) and such repetition makes achievement of spontaneity very difficult indeed, not only for the actor speaking the lines, but also for the actor listening to them.

Perhaps the best way to arrive at a freshness of approach with each succeeding take is to listen afresh, to look for possibly unnoticed nuances in the readings or the physical attitudes of the

*Every student of acting should study Jack Lemmon's performance in the film, *Missing*. One careful viewing is worth a month of exercises. Here is attention at its highest level. The intensity of his listening and watching is awesome. His bodily movements and attitudes are also something to study; these aspects of acting are discussed in a later chapter.

other player (or players). Unless he is an extremely mechanical actor (in which case he shouldn't be working in films) the player will usually have some variation, however slight, in each take. And it is that variation the listening actor should be looking for.

Willie Wyler had a reputation for shooting innumerable takes of every scene, though he would rarely if ever tell the actors involved what nuance he was seeking. He was actualy relying on their doing "something different" instinctively in every take, and when that something "different" was something "right," Wyler had his desired take.

Of course, the something different also brings out a different reaction, but even if the speaker essentially repeats his earlier performances, the very effort of looking for something new will serve to divert the actor's attention from the problem of repetition, to direct it toward the possibilities of change rather than the deadliness of rote.

*　*　*

The actress speaks:

When our picture was finished and in the theaters, this is the way the audience saw that scene. As my sister starts her tirade against me, I'm seated on the couch (a group shot). The audience watches her face, but as I rise and start walking around, it also watches my movements. At one point I turn to her and break into her speech with a line. They cut to a close shot of me as I start speaking then, halfway through, they cut to a matching close shot of my sister listening to me. They stay on her while she starts her answer, letting the audience digest her words, then cut to a close shot of me listening. The audience listens with me while watching me fall apart as my sister's words expose me for the child that I am, and make me face the unattractive truth of what I have done. The tears collect in my eyes and start rolling down my cheeks. I start my last line, but I don't need to finish it—I have to turn and run out. Good scene. Excellently directed. Superbly cut.

On this particular film, with this director, I became aware more than ever before of the importance of listening, of keeping the audience aware of your feelings at all times. The "scene stealer" is an actor who keeps the viewer's eyes on him every minute he is on the screen, no matter what else is being done or who is doing it. The expert scene stealer does this without making enemies of the rest of the cast. It isn't necessary to do anything more than what comes naturally.

The point is, the director shoots a large part of the scene in several different set-ups—group shots, over-the-shoulder shots, and close shots—of exactly the same dialogue. And an actor can't be certain which shots will be used; even the director probably doesn't know at this point. He will decide when he has seen them all. But you must never let yourself get out of character from the minute he calls "Action!" A professional, a really good actor, plays it all the way and gives the other actors someone to play to.

Making a film is a collective effort of the entire cast and crew. If one person fails in his job the film is in jeopardy. The crew— electricians, gaffers, prop men, makeup, hairdresser, and ward-robe personnel—all are there to help you to look good on the screen. This does not make you more important. They expect you to do your job well so that they can be proud of their work. And if you behave in a professional manner (on time, know your lines, be ready, and don't hold anyone up) you will be well liked, joked with, and treated as one of them. This makes for a happy company when the cast and crew look forward to each day's working together.

Confinement to space and marks bothers some actors in the beginning, but you can get used to this during rehearsals. You can hit your marks without ever looking down, by becoming aware of the location of people and/or furniture close to your stopping points. You can help the cameraman by feeling your light and watching shadows during rehearsal, and the other actors will appreciate knowing you are aware of their lights.

To be comfortable with your part, your character, is number one. Number two is to feel at home on the set with the crew. This gives you the added confidence and support you need, so that when all the stage lights go out and only you are lit for the scene, the transition is smooth—not a worry in the world.

The faces of Rhonda Fleming, Regis Toomey, Dick Powell and Richard Erdman are waiting for a reaction from Jean Porter caught pick-pocketing in Cry Danger.

5

Make a Face

Sometimes it pays to go back to basics, to define our terms.

React: to be moved to action in response to an influence or a particular stimulus.

Stimulus: something that incites to action or exertion.

Two of the world's leading actors, Laurence Olivier and Alec Guinness, have recently indulged in some loose talk, or they have been misquoted. Each has reportedly said that screen acting is, in effect, "doing nothing." Such a statement may be simply a display of excessive modesty, a caution against "acting," or over-playing, or it may be meant as a comparison of the relative intensities of acting for the stage or the screen, but I refuse to believe that it was intended to be taken literally. Certainly, listening and observing are not "doing nothing." Nor is proper reacting.

It has often been said that reacting is the essence of acting for the screen, and by definition, to react is to respond to a particular stimulus. The stimulus, whether it be an idea, an emotion (like anticipation, fear, or grief), or the brain's recognition of a physical sensation like hunger, thirst, or an itch, may be generated within the actor himself. More often, perhaps, the stimulus comes from the outside, from another character in the scene or from some circumstance or combination of circumstances outside the actor's control. There may even be more than one stimulus, leading to contradictory reactions and eventual *in*action. But the stimulus is always a positive force, even when it results in an indecisive or a negative response.

It necessarily follows that responding to stimuli is a continuous, an on-going, activity. As long as consciousness is present, it never stops. And, it must never be allowed to stop on the screen.

From a director's point of view, the response to a stimulus (commonly calleld a reaction) is perhaps the most important element in a film.* Every competent director searches his script for those moments that make the film move, and movement is impossible without change, whether physical or mental. Each change or transition alters the course of the character's subsequent actions, thus enriching the plot and keeping the film alive.

The viewer recognizes a transition only through the player's reaction. A response to some physical action is easily understood, but a reaction to a new idea or intention, as expressed in a line of dialogue, is much more difficult to realize. The line itself rarely shows a transition, since it is usually the pronouncement of a change already made in the speaker's mind; it merely states a position and is therefore static. The listener's reaction to the stated idea contained in the line shows us the change in progress, which is dynamic.

I must emphasize here that the physical manifestation of a reaction, no matter how important, should not be exaggerated. "Broad" reactions are occasionally called for but, on the screen, the subtle reaction is usually the best, even in comedy. Our greatest comedians, men like Chaplin, Keaton, and Langdon, contrived broad, sometimes wild, situations, but their reactions were usually remarkably subtle.

In dialogue scenes the reaction is almost always triggered while the actor is listening. The trigger that stimulates the response rarely comes, like a word cue, at the end of the line. It comes at the moment the sense of the line becomes apparent, and if that is obvious early on, as is frequently the case, the response will come well before the triggering line is completed. Such a reaction

---

*The failure to understand this sinks many screen writers. They are satisfied to write the lines that provide the stimulus, but take the reaction for granted. In fact, the reaction is much more important than the line that stimulates it.

is usually visual, but when it is accompanied by a vocal response, the result is a natural interruption.

A brief aside. Some years ago, writers realized that an actor could step on another actor's lines; that, in fact, it was not only a more honest, more realistic reaction, but it was often more dramatic. That realization led to an interesting script-writing convention: most dialogue was designed as a series of open-ended or unfinished lines that were meant to be stepped on. However, in order to protect the integrity of his dialogue, however, a writer would still write the complete line, then add a few sacrificial words—an incomplete phrase—that the responding actor could interrupt while leaving the original line in the clear. But, since the proper reaction was still inspired by the proper stimulus (somewhere in the original line), the responding actor was forced to delay his response artificially for an additional and unreasonable length of time. This was dishonest, destroying reality and the scene's pace and rhythm. I believe this convention is now used only sparingly, if at all. It is far better for an actor to find and fix his own timing when confronted by the need for an overlapping reaction.

The best reactions are a natural result of paying attention, and they should be inborn and simple. Except in broad comedy or when contriving a deception, there is never any need to manufacture a visual response—to "make a face"—as demonstrated in the dim past by close-up photographs of "fear," "desire," "lust," "pain," and the like. On the screen the camera accentuates reaction by magnifying the source, and the closer the shot the greater the need for limiting the reaction to the eyes alone. The honest reaction in life is usually a controlled one; broad reactions, unless gradually approached, immediately label the reactor an extreme neurotic or a fraud. Even reactions, or, I should say, particularly reactions to extreme stimuli such as an announcement of death or sudden infliction of pain must be very carefully considered.

As a rule, the immediate broad reaction to the announcement, "He's dead!" is very artificial and is so perceived by the viewer. The human brain and body usually react to such a crisis with a traumatic shock that temporarily prevents understanding and acceptance of the situation, and diminishes or stops altogether any immediate emotional response. The same is true for extreme pain, as anyone who has suffered a severe accident can testify. The shock of such a trauma often prevents the victim from even being aware that an injury has occurred.

Of course, not all reactions are quick or overlapping. When the sense of a spoken line is purposely obscure or (rarely) profound, the reaction must be extended and the subsequent vocal response delayed. If the meaning of such a line is intended to be grasped by the viewer, he must be given time to riddle it out, and he can get that required time only if the player's visual reaction is arbitrarily prolonged. This may pose a difficult acting problem.

The actor, because of prolonged script study and rehearsal, knows the line and its meaning thoroughly, and will frequently shorten his reaction and respond vocally before the viewer, who is hearing the line for the first time, can fully grasp its significance. It must always be kept in mind that, in a film, there is no leafing back to refresh one's memory, to restudy a statement. If the meaning is meant to be understood it must be made clear the first time around, and the viewer must be given the time to absorb and analyze the given information. Obviously, it is preferable that the actor (with the help of the director) should estimate the time needed for such understanding and supply it through an extended reaction.*

However, if the actor exhibits conscious awareness of the timing requirement, such a reaction will appear to be contrived. Just as he must conquer the problem of repetition in the interest of spontaneity, so he must solve the problem of arbitrarily imposed timing for the sake of audience understanding. The best way to block out such preperformance awareness is to listen to the line in question as if it were a puzzler whose meaning is more complex than he had anticipated. Even if the complexity is not present, the listener's search for it requires the addition of an extra beat to the reaction. That beat allows the viewer to catch up with the actor in his understanding.

---

*As a film editor I have, on a number of occasions, found it necessary to lengthen over-quick reactions by the use of special techniques (see Dmytryk On FILM EDITING. Boston: Focal Press, 1984, Chapter 10).

*   *   *

The actress speaks:

Study the stars.

Yes, even look to the heavens for help. Many of our great screen actors and actresses are gone, but we can be thankful to the film people who have protected and preserved their works. Watch old movies on TV. Look for special programs at museums. In most cities you'll find at least one theater manager who realizes that many people enjoy the old movies, the big stars.

Ladies, study Marlene Dietrich, Joan Crawford, Bette Davis, Ingrid Bergman. Oh, there are more, but these greats come quickly to mind because each had a style of her own that made her a star. It's easy to impersonate any one of these women, and in doing just that you can see what kept them in the limelight for so long.

For instance, pretend you are Dietrich, standing in a court-room, favoring camera right, and someone speaks to you from camera left. Have you noticed how her eyes always move in the direction she is going to turn before she ever moves her head or her body? This is an important effect for the screen. I've often wondered how she discovered it. In fact, it's delicious! She always does it. It gives her time before she starts her next line. With it she captures the audience, then holds it throughout the scene, just with this effect. Her eyes move as far as they can to the left, then her head slowly turns until she locks eyes with her opponent or lover. Get it? Practice it. Most often you will find that your mouth will open slightly as you turn your head, just as hers did.

And how about Joan Crawford? She snapped her head in response most of the time. She was famous for her snappy retorts. Pretend you are Crawford, standing in a courtroom, favoring camera right, and someone speaks to you from camera left. The moment the line is finished she snaps her head and looks directly into the speaker's eyes, then starts her line. This, too, grabs the audience. With flashing eyes she is on fire, and viewers are with her all the way. Bette Davis was also famous for this attack, even in love scenes.

Bergman—study the way she looks into the eyes of her lover, pulling her eyes up from the floor; study her steadiness and her passion. Have you watched her nostrils during a love scene? Yes! Her nostils widen and close, widen and close, as she becomes more passionate. Acting? Yes, and only for the screen. Only the camera can pick up nostril action, and believe me, it's an emotional jolt.

Men, study Bogie, Gable, Bill Powell, Spencer Tracy, and Jack Lemon. Here again, others come to mind, but these greats had and have such style, each with his own personality, of course, and also a trick or two. Bogie seems always to be studying the face of whoever he is working opposite. Whether playing a lover or a heavy, his eyes shift and search for information from his coactor. With this tenseness, he makes you so aware of his emotions that you know what he's going to do before he does it (a smack on the lips or a smack in the face). And isn't he marvelous when he fools you, turning his back, walking out on the woman to whom he has just said beautiful things.

Gable. What can you say about the King who became a fine actor after he was a star? His looks and personality made him a star and then he realized that to hold on to stardom he'd better learn really how to act. In an interview, he once credited Spencer Tracy with showing him the way to relaxed easiness and more naturalness.

Tracy was the master at that. I don't believe he ever realized how great he was on the screen. He was a writer's dream. Spence could take any line, sometimes exactly as written, or with just a slight change, and make it sound as though it had just come to mind. With pauses, thinking on camera, he could convince an audience of anything.

Bill Powell started out playing heavies and switched to comedy, which made him a star. His sophisticated, clean look (even while playing a drunk) was the key, so he set his timing to fit his character.

Jack Lemmon is an excellent actor to study. To me, he is the perfect screen actor, from his toes to the top of his head. He can make you weep as he walks away, his back to the camera, his shoulders slumped and his walk slowed. You pull for him to look back at you; he pauses briefly, but continues on. Study Jack Lemmon, especially in Missing and The China Syndrome. He listens on-camera better than anyone I've ever seen.

All of this is to help you understand what screen acting entails. What makes a good screen actor. What makes a star.

And it doesn't hurt to steal a little here and there if you see something you can use to help develop your own style. Be good, but be unique.

Jean Porter plays Humphrey Bogart's Chinese girlfriend in Left Hand of God.

6

What Did He Say?

Film is an eclectic medium; there is nothing like it in the field of the arts. It can deliver a play, a ballet, a symphony, an opera, or a sermon; it can feature poetic dialogue or punk rock music, movement of various types and tempos, and even pictorial works of art.* It can present a classic tragedy or the broadest kind of comedy. In short, it can duplicate the works of any other field of art and often range beyond them. What other medium can give you *Nanook of the North, The Man of Aran, The Bridge on the River Kwai, The Year of Living Dangerously, Chariots of Fire;* the action of *Bullit* or *The French Connection;* or the stark drama of the "Odessa Steps" sequence from *The Battleship Potemkin?*

This tiny selection, picked at random, exemplifies what many consider the best aspects of the medium—films deliver their messages through the effective use of faces, reactions, attitudes, and movement rather than through dialogue.

I mention this here because I believe (together with many others) that the modern film, especially as seen on the TV screen, has fallen on dull times. For a number of reasons, largely economic, most films today are merely a tiresome succession of talking heads. In other words, with only rare exceptions, today's films are plays, and not very good plays at that.

---

*Regardless of the quality of its subject matter, a well-shot film offers dozens of beautifully composed "pictures," though these may last for a few seconds only.

There is nothing wicked in filming a good play. *Becket* and *A Man for All Seasons* come to mind as excellent and eminently watchable films. But to persist in filming plays is to continue using only a part of the screen's potential as art and entertainment. I think the film public deserves less talk and more movie.

The concentration on talking heads also does a disservice to students of acting. It tends to divert attention away from the kind of acting the best films require, the kind that has been discussed in the preceding chapters. Importance is centered on reading lines, since that is by far the greatest concern of the average film. But the handling of dialogue is by no means the most important aspect of acting for the screen—for several reasons.

To begin with, a truly objective reading of a good script will show that relatively few speeches are vitally important from a dramatic point of view. A large number of lines are throw-aways, that is, they do little to further the plot, they have no philosophical relevance, and generally no poetic beauty. Nor, as a rule, should they. Good plot construction is best accomplished through the proper development of the characters' reactions, and subsequent actions, to well-conceived crises (major or minor) and conflicts. Intellectual or philosophical relevance depends on the revealed depths of the characters and the dramatic presentation of their behavioral choices. And, for reasons to be discussed presently, most films have little use for vocal poetry, though there may be "poetry" in visual beauty and in human behavior.

An actor who uses an earth-shaking delivery when speaking a simple line is very pretentious indeed, yet I have known well-established players who have spoken a casual, "Good evening," as if they were declaiming, " 'Tis the witching hour of night . . ." The tendency toward this kind of elocution arises from the actor's inordinate respect for the written word. This not uncommon affliction is shared by a great many people who have no acting experience at all. But the actor, at least, should have an easy-going, casual relationship with words and lines, as he has with anygood friends or old acquaintances.

Let us consider the sanctity of the written word. There is, of course, no such thing. These days even the King James version of the *Holy Bible* is being rewritten every month or so, and if you can rewrite God, you can certainly rewrite any author who ever lived.

This should not be taken as a recommendation that every actor immediately start rewriting his current script or, in fact, that any actor should do so. What I do suggest is that the actor analyze his lines carefully, judging their relative values, their consistencies, and their dramatic legitimacy.

Is a particular line meant to be casual or does it carry a good deal of weight? If it is meant to be important, is it too obviously pretentious? If it is meant to be casual, is it so written? A casual line can pose a number of problems. It can be overbearing, presuming more importance than it should honestly possess, it may be worded in a stilted manner, or it may be too "literary."

The casual line should not be lightly regarded, but studied as thoroughly as any other line in a film. If it belongs at all, it obviously serves a purpose, and though that purpose may be relatively unimportant, it is a necessary part of the whole and must be treated with respect. A throw-away that has a purpose is often more difficult to master than pretentious dialogue. Some rather good actors have had trouble delivering the casual line. (I am convinced that Spencer Tracy's much admired reputation as an underplayer rested on his unbelievable mastery of the casual line.)

Casualness does not imply indistinctness. Oddly, a line that cannot be understood gains in importance. The viewer hates to miss anything, and since he cannot know the indistinct line was of little real consquence, he will assume it is something he should have heard. A feeling of frustration or irritation inevitably follows. There are exceptions, of course. A well-known adage or a frequently repeated line can be sloughed off without damage since its meaning is immediately clear. In fact, it is often better purposely to slur such a line. For instance, an actor can say, "A butcher, a baker, a-DA-da-da-da," and everyone in the audience over the age of three will be well ahead of him. But in the great majority of instances it is the manner, the attitude, or the intonation that should distinguish the casual throw-away, not lack of intelligibility.

A study of the casual line brings out an important aspect of dialogue in general—*spoken* dialogue can, and usually does, differ considerably from *written* dialogue. A line, mentally absorbed off the page, may seem to be quite natural. Yet when spoken aloud, that same line will sound awkward and unreal. This should come as no surprise. Until very recently the conventions of the

written word differed widely from those of conversational usage.*
Even today, in many languages, writing in the vernacular is un-
acceptable.

I have known very few authors who could write truly honest
speaking dialogue. I do not mean this as a criticism, but as a
statement of fact. I, myself, have written many a line of dialogue
that I considered strikingly natural, but which, on being spoken,
sounded more than a trifle starchy. For anyone brought up and
educated in our society, such difficulties are practically inevitable. The final test of a line's authenticity is always in the speaking, not the reading.

However, and this is a very important however, it is essential
that the validity of a line be judged by its relationship to the
character who says it, not the actor who speaks it. One of an
actor's most baseless complaints is, "I wouldn't say it that way."
Of course not. Even though an actor brings himself to every part
he plays, the self he brings has most probably been reared differently, educated differently, has associated with different kinds
of people in a different environment; it is the character, with his
distinctive rearing and conditioning, who is speaking the line,
not the actor. The only valid criticism would be, "I don't think
the character would say it that way," and such a judgment would,
of course, be debatable. Its final disposition is usually decided by
the film's director.

But back to dialogue. Written dialogue is a finished product;
in real life most spoken dialogue is ad lib. The screenplay writer
is often casual or off-hand with his scene descriptions, since he
assumes that the director will construct and stage the scenes his
(the director's) way. But he slaves over every spoken line since
these, he fully expects, will be delivered more or less as written.
He edits, reconstructs, and polishes most of his dialogue, and he
is correct in doing so. As in most art, the scene is the essence of
a happening, not the happening itself. Two buddies planning a
fishing trip might spend hours discussing it—the writer must
wrap it up in at most a page or two.

But too often the process of selecting and miniaturizing dia-

---

*For this reason it is very difficult to guess how the language of, say, the
eighteenth century was spoken, and patterning dialogue after the literature of
the period invariably results in stilted, corny speech.

logue succeeds in achieving a result identical to the dehydration of fruits or vegetables—a desiccated husk. The actor must find a way of giving that husk some appropriate flesh. (This is an exaggeration, of course, but I hope it makes the point.) The line of dialogue in a script is usually properly constructed and polished, the thought is quite complete. Would it were so in real life.

Few people speak in polished, well-constructed, completely thought-out sentences, at least not when they ad lib. And the actor's job is to make the character real, to make his manner of behaving and speaking believable. To do this he must often take liberties with the written words. He might stutter a little (clod-kicking often makes speeches, as well as characters, appear to be more natural)* or he may leave a portion of the line hanging, since rarely are one's thoughts positive and complete. He may repeat a word, even a phrase, in order to capture that uncertainty most speakers exhibit when vocally expressing an incompletely framed idea. He may decide (with the director's approval or at his suggestion) to substitute a colloquial word or phrase for a more polite one, and always, unless he is playing a pedantic or a pompous personality, he will try to approach the vernacular.

It is inconceivable that an actor can become a good actor by simply learning to speak properly. He must necessarily develop a keen ear for speech—other people's speech. He must be able to duplicate (not as imitation, but quite naturally) their speaking mannerisms, both oral and physical. He must learn their vocal graces and their vocal tics. He must be able to recognize the sound of truth and to detect the sound of deception so he can incorporate these sounds into the speech of his character. He can do this only if he spends a good deal of his learning time in watching and listening to people—people from every walk of life. Just as a master impressionist studies the famous in order to caricature them effectively, so the actor must study the not-so-famous in order to portray them truthfully.

*I once stopped Spencer Tracy in the middle of a take. "What's the matter?" he asked. "Spence," I said, "you're hemming and hawing a little too much." "Mr. Director," he shot back, seriocomically, "I am very highly paid for hemming and hawing." And even though we agreed that in this particular instance he was overdoing that bit, in general, he was quite right. Nobody could bumble a line as effectively as the great Tracy.

Such study and learning should lead not to imitation but to creation. For example, a character may be patterned after a person who speaks in a slovenly fashion, so sloppily that only his close relatives and most intimate friends can understand him. Obviously, a faithful reproduction of such speaking habits would be gibberish to viewers unaccustomed to such speech. Above all, most of a film's dialogue is meant to be understood. So, a compromise is in order, one that is not truly a compromise but also a reconstruction. Certain elements must be selected that project the essence of the character's sloppy speech without rendering it un-understandable.

In *A Streetcar Named Desire,* Marlon Brando created such a speech pattern so effectively that many knowledgeable people wondered whether he could ever do a straight part without mumbling. Obviously, he could and did; mumbling was not, and is not, a part of Brando's normal speech pattern. It was an exceptional creative effort, made thoroughly real by an exceptional artist.

In short, an ear for the nature and the meaning of the lyrics and a facility for phrasing are more important than the strict melody. The good actor must be able to "do something with it."

The quality of an actor's voice is obviously of great importance, as is his basic accent. A nasal whine can be repellent, but so can a vocal quality previously much admired in actors and orators— sonorousness. Resonance may be needed to reach the balcony; it can only be a problem for a microphone a few inches away. On the screen, the sonorous actor sounds pompous and ostentatious, and is effective only if he is playing Colonel Blimp or Senator Claghorn.

Voice quality and placement can usually be improved with practice and the aid of an inexpensive tape recorder. A marked regional accent can be lost and, indeed, it should be. The possession of, let us say, a strong Brooklyn accent may be useful when called for in a particular character, but it severely limits an actor's range and acting opportunities if it remains a permanent feature.

Not too long after World War II, when English films were making a splash on the American market, I heard Olivier, John Mills, and a couple of other British actors discussing the question of the English accent, which many Americans found difficult to understand. They were able to agree that strong affectations were undesirable for aesthetic as well as commercial reasons. Thus was born what has since been called the "mid-Atlantic" accent, a reasonable (and pleasing) compromise between the American and British treatments of the King's English.

In the United States at present, television is undoubtedly affecting our own speech patterns, and though regional purists may decry the "anchor man" manner of speech, it is really the only way for an actor to go. The use of the neutral, essentially unaffected accent now prevalent in certain parts of the midwest and most of the Pacific Coast makes it easier for the actor to superimpose any desired local accent over his normal one. Just imagine how difficult it would be to speak New England if your basic speech patterns came by way of West Texas.

A few actors still shout, or at least speak much too loudly. Most modern actors, however, have learned that the microphone can easily handle anything down to a soft sigh; stage whispers have no place on the screen except as a source of comedy. But by no means have all modern actors learned whom to talk to. Some, in a sense, tale to the mike. Even though they know they can talk as quietly as they wish, they still speak their lines for their effect on the audience. This is inexcusable because it is still declaiming, no matter how quietly. Conversations between human beings are only rarely declamatory.

Unless he is screaming at the wind, the actor should say what he has to say to the person or persons he is supposed to be talking to. Whether he is shouting, speaking in measured tones, or whispering, whether he is looking at them or avoiding their eyes, he should direct his words to his on-screen listeners. Only then will he be a real person and not a performer. It is up to the director, the cameraman, the sound mixer, and the cutter to bring those words to an audience; it is not up to the actor.

Try an experiment. Speak any long monlogue as you might speak it in a theater (if possible, record it on tape). Then speak it confidentially to a person standing or sitting no more than four or five feet away from you. The difference will astound you and, I hope, convince you of the superiority, at least in films, of talking to your coactors rather than to the audience.

*   *   *

The actress speaks:

*Motion picture scripts are rarely written exactly as they should
be spoken. I've seen a few writers try it and it just doesn't work.
A favorite writer of mine, Jimmy Clavell, once wrote a script
with several different accents, plus the descriptions of how he
saw the actors reacting, and it was the funniest thing I've ever
read. I think it was his first try. He also laughed at it, all the
way to the bank with the takings from his second try. He's never
stopped laughing and writing and making money, but he did
stop writing accents and directions.*

*Take the script given you and make the part yours. As you
read and learn the lines, you may find you have to change them
just a bit to suit your own portrayal of the character. The director
and the writer will appreciate this as long as your changes make
it better. But don't go too far.*

*For instance, here is a scene as exactly written from Alfred
Hayes script of* The Left Hand of God, *in which I played Mary
Yin, Humphrey Bogart's Chinese girlfriend. Bogie's character was
called Jim Carmody.*

11   INT. CARMODY'S ROOM—FULL SHOT—LATE AFTERNOON

A big, square chamber, old, elegant and warmly lit. Right, a single
huge log burns in a stone fireplace. In the corners are four brass
lanterns in soot-stained niches. Left, a modern desk with a green-
shaded oil lamp whose light falls far enough to show Mary Yin,
provocatively stretched out on Carmody's bed in f.g. Footsteps
are heard, but Mary Yin continues to stare at the ceiling. Carmody, dust-worn, appears in the door in b.g.. He stares and waits.
Her not looking up is as deliberate as a pose before a mirror, for
Mary Yin is as aware of Carmody as he is of her.

CARMODY
(finally, with a grin)
All right, Mary Yin—change the pose. I forgot
my camera.

She looks at him slowly, deliberately, then smiles.

(continued)

11 (continued)

> ### MARY YIN
> After so many days of hard riding, I thought
> to see me this way would be restful.

With a tantalizing movement of her body, she rises and saunters
across the room, aware of his gaze trailing her slow passage.
She is an exquisite half-caste. Little gold sandals glitter as she
walks, dark blue silken trousers ripple provocatively. She arrives
at the liquor cabinet.

> ### CARMODY
> (meanwhile)
> You're a lot of things, but restful isn't one of
> them.

Holding whiskey bottle and glass, she turns poutingly.

> ### MARY YIN
> It's been lonely without you, Kah-ma-dee.
> There was nobody to play the piano.

> ### CARMODY
> What's the matter with the radio?

Mary Yin brings the drink to Carmody.

> ### MARY YIN
> (with a shrug)
> You know Yang. Nobody ever turns off the
> radio here. All the batteries are dead.
> (hands him the drink)
> Tell me what you did in the hills.

12   CLOSE TWO SHOT—CARMODY AND MARY YIN—LATE
        AFTERNOON

> ### CARMODY
> I spent six days collecting Yang's taxes . . .

He takes a long drink, then walks over to the desk, putting down
his cap, the Bible, and his whip. Mary Yin stays in the b.g.

> ### MARY YIN
> (somewhat eagerly)
> Did you fight?

(continued)

12 (continued)

                            CARMODY
            Dust—insects—the mountains . . .
                       (looking at her)
            Disappointed?

                            MARY YIN
                    (crossing to him)
            A little.

As she reaches the desk she notices the priest's Bible. It is dust covered. She picks it up, curiously, as an object completely alien to this room

                            MARY YIN
            That's odd. A Bible. Where did you get this?

                            CARMODY
                   (a slight shrug)
            A hotel room in Chicago.
                   (takes the Bible,
                   puts it down again
                   on the table)
            Now beat it. Yang's waiting for me to check in.

                            MARY YIN
            You haven't kissed me.
                   (her face close
                   to his)
            It's so dull here when you're gone.

He takes her somewhat roughly and kisses her hard.

                            CARMODY
                   (breaking away and crossing
                   with empty glass toward
                   liquor cabinet)
            You should have stayed in Chungking.

                            MARY YIN
            Why?

13   MED. SHOT AT LIQUOR CABINET—LATE AFTERNOON

As he reaches for the bottle.

(continued)

13 (continued)

>CARMODY

It's not dull—and it's twenty days nearer the coast.

He fills the glass. Mary Yin comes into shot.

>MARY YIN

Are you so tired of China?

>CARMODY
>(looking into his
>glass)

For three years I've run Yang's tin army. You can get tired of anything in three years.

>MARY YIN
>(softly)

Poor Kah-ma-dee.

>MARY YIN (cont.)
>(as he looks at her)

Other men would envy what you have.

>CARMODY

This?

>(a gesture at the
>elaborate room)

You buy stuff like this at auction.

>MARY YIN
>(caressing)

Could I be bought at auction, too?

>CARMODY
>(a crooked smile)

Sure, if they're selling calendars.

He breaks away. She catches his arm.

>MARY YIN

Why did you come back to China—if you hate it so?

>CARMODY
>(a shrug)

Money.

(continued)

13 (continued)

> **MARY YIN**
>
> Yang pays you plenty. If it's money you
> want—
>
> **CARMODY**
>
> Money, plus.
> > (as she frowns)
>
> What does Jan Teng call it? The illusion of
> freedom. Out there's . . .
> > (a gesture toward
> > the window)
>
> . . . the biggest prison in the world. The
> accommodations are fine—but every night I
> can hear them turn the key in the lock.
> > (he swallows the
> > remainder of his drink)
>
> Now beat it. Yang likes his boys punctual.

He turns, and again she catches his arm.

> **MARY YIN**
> > (sweetly)
>
> So do I, Kah-ma-dee.

Camera holds on her as he strides out of shot.

*Reads okay, doesn't it? But can you see what I mean when I
suggest a writer should not write accents, leaving it to the actor
instead? I was playing a Chinese girl living in China in wartime.
I had Chinese friends to study but they were modern Califor-
nians, so I recalled some of the research I had done at M.G.M.
While under contract there I was tested to play a part in* Dragon
Seed. *The part was "Little Pearl," a young girl in Katherine Hep-
burn's family. Dickie Jones was to play my brother. While testing
Bill Tuttle's fine makeup creations, I went through Metro's film
library and looked at all the Chinese films I could get my hands
on. I started thinking, walking, and talking Chinese. I got the
part, then it was cut out. How about that?! All of the preparatory
work down the drain. Well, at Fox, on this film, I was able to
make use of it.*

*If the screen writer thought it necessary to write the way he
felt Mary Yin should pronounce Carmody's name—Kah-ma-dee—
why not be consistent and write her complete lines with his idea
of a Chinese accent?*

What I did with all the lines was a "soft sell." It just so happened that Kah-ma-dee fit perfectly with the rest of my dialogue. Chinese shorten most of their words; when speaking English each word is cut almost like their chop-chop language. (Don't get me wrong, Chang. I love it!) But for the character I was playing, I had to make certain she was clearly understood, with all the mannerisms men like to think are Oriental. What they really are is Feminine, with a capital F.

So for the dialogue I made sure my voice stayed sweet and soft, almost purring.

Speaking of purring, the scene did not begin as written. Instead of just lying on the bed staring at the ceiling, the director had me playing with a couple of Siamese kittens. Worked much better.

The director and Bogie and I worked well together, and the following changes were decided on, on the set.

Half of my second line was cut ("There was nobody to play the piano"), as was Bogie's next and half of my next. So it went . . .

MARY YIN

It's been lonely without you, Kah-ma-dee. Tell
me what you did in the hills.

That was a relief to me because I had not been able to fathom the piano and radio and battery stuff in Chinese.

Further into the scene we cut out the action and the two lines relating to her finding the Bible on his desk. So it went from Mary Yin's line . . .

MARY YIN

A little.
(she moves into him
and continues)
You haven't kissed me.
(moves her face close)
It's so dull when you're gone.

He takes her somewhat roughly and kisses her hard.

I repeated this descriptive action for a reason.

How many of you ladies have ever wished Humphrey Bogart would grab you somewhat roughly and kiss you hard!

Well, I was one of you! As a teenager sitting in the balcony of the Hollywood Boulevard Warner Bros. Theater, watching Humphrey Bogart in The Maltese Falcon, *I nearly chewed up the upholstery wishing I could be up there on the screen, in his arms. I melted as he kissed Mary Astor. And let me tell you—and this came as a shock—I nearly melted when he kissed me as the Chinese girl.*

By this time Bogie and his wife, Betty Bacall, and I were friends, and my husband was directing the film. But for one long moment (and it was a long moment because my darling husband, as a joke, decided to leave us in the clinch for as long as we could hold it), for that one brief moment, I was able to forget Bacall and Eddie and the rest of the world.

So there you are. How funny life is. A dream comes true every once in a while. Especially in Hollywood.

The scene as rewritten, ran as follows: (cuts and description are left out since a scene is rarely staged or cut according to script, and the director changed a couple of Bogart's lines.)

CARMODY
(finally, with a grin)
All right, Mary Yin—change the pose. I forgot
my camera.

She looks at him slowly, deliberately, then smiles.

MARY YIN
After so many days of hard riding, I thought
to see me this way would be restful.

CARMODY
You're a lot of things, but restful isn't one of
them.

MARY YIN
It's been lonely without you, Kah-ma-dee. Tell
me what you did in the hills.

CARMODY
I spent six days collecting Yang's taxes—and
a sore behind.

(continued)

(continued)

> ### MARY YIN
> (somewhat eagerly)

Did you fight?

> ### CARMODY

Dust—insects—the mountains . . .
> (looking at her)

Disappointed?

> ### MARY YIN

A little.
> (she moves into him and continues)

You haven't kissed me.
> (moves her face close)

It's so dull when you're gone.

He takes her somewhat roughly and kisses her hard.

> ### CARMODY
> (breaking away)

You should have stayed in Chungking.

> ### MARY YIN

Why?

> ### CARMODY

It's not dull—and it's twenty days nearer the
coast.

> ### MARY YIN

Are you so tired of China?

> ### CARMODY

For three years I've run Yang's tin army. You
can get tired of anything in three years.

> ### MARY YIN
> (softly)

Poor Kah-ma-dee.
> (as he looks at her)

Other men would envy what you have.

> ### CARMODY

This?
> (a gesture at the
> elaborate room)

You buy stuff like this at auction.

(continued)

(continued)

                              MARY YIN
                            (caressing)
                Could I be bought at auction, too?

                              CARMODY
                         (a crooked smile)
                Sure, if they're selling calendars.

                              MARY YIN
                Why did you come back to China—if you hate
                it so?

                              CARMODY
                            (a shrug)

                Money.

                              MARY YIN
                Yang pays you plenty. If it's money you
                want—

                              CARMODY
                I've found out there's something else.
                            (as she frowns)
                What does Jan Teng call it? The illusion of
                freedom. Out there's . . .
                        (a gesture toward
                         the window)
                . . . the biggest prison in the world. The
                accommodations are fine—but every night I
                can hear them turn the key in the lock.
                        (he swallows the remainder
                         of his drink)
                Now beat it. Yang likes his boys puctual.

                              MARY YIN
                            (sweetly)
                So do I, Kah-ma-dee.

        Caeera holds on her as he strides out of shot.

*Today they would use Chinese actors for Chinese parts, and
I think they should. I played Robert Walker's French girlfriend
(living in a small French wartime village) in M.G.M.'s* What
Next, Corporal Hargrove. *I had to study French for many weeks,
and watch* The Big Parade *over and over. Metro had a great film
library, and all the contract players were encouraged to use it.
I was very fortunate.*

But you can be, too. Film is so popular today, and it is certainly recognized as the world's number-one art form for reaching the largest number of people. In any large city, if one cares to look, there are museums and libraries with old films for study.

Edward Dmytryk directs Jane Fonda in Walk on the Wild Side.

7

Who Do You Think You Are?

We were casting *Murder My Sweet*. One actor, fresh from New York, frequently dropped into my office. He wanted, oh, so desperately, to play Moose Malloy. The conversation always followed a pattern; perhaps he though he could wear me down.

"You're five feet nine," I would say. "The Moose is supposed to be six feet eight inches tall."

"I can *play* it big!" he would plead. But he didn't get the part. Mike Mazurki, the wrestler, at six feet four and a half inches the biggest man we could find who could act, got the role. Dick Powell, who played Marlow, was six feet two, so even with Mazurki as the Moose I had to use every trick in the book to get an on-screen difference in height that was dramatically effective.

As Edward G. Robinson and James Cagney demonstrated so convincingly, power can be played regardless of size, but height cannot be acted. As for tricks, there's a limit to the build-up position of a pair of men's shoes.

It is a mistake to assume that any actor can divorce himself completely from the screen character he is playing. To do that he would have to change every personal characteristic as well as every personal habit. But habits are the result of a lifetime of conditioning, and they can be broken or temporarily changed only by the application of constant conscious effort. Yet the chief characteristic of a habit is that it is an unconscious or involuntary action or reaction. A person does not think about how he picks up a fork at dinner or how he brushes his teeth or combs his hair, and it would be impossible to change one's whole exterior and interior way of coping with the daily demands of one's environment in the limited time available prior to an actual performance. The effort would be bound to show.

A small number of actors who seem to value technique as an end in itself do attempt such transformations (introverted movements of this sort have cropped up at various times in all of the arts). But they attract only a minute audience with an extremely esoteric outlook. To most viewers their efforts appear to be self-conscious and self-indulgent.

With this in mind, it would seem to be wise for the actor to bring as much of himself to his screen character as that character can accommodate, and to avoid most attempts at "creating" characters whose involuntary habits and attitudes are the reverse of the actor's own. It would be sheer nonsense, for instance, for Robert Redford to play Scrooge, for James Garner to play the Godfather, or for Al Pacino to play a sweet-talking seminary student. In keeping with the old theater belief that comedians always want to be tragedians (and vice versa), such attempts might seem attractive to the artists but they rarely, if ever, turn out to be attractive at the box office. A number of such extreme character reversals have been attempted*; the results have been more tragic than the films.

Let us set up a specific example, and imagine that Jack Nicholson is cast to play a blacksmith. How much of the character would be some hypothetical "Blacksmith" and how much would be Jack Nicholson?

At this point I can hear some reader saying, "But Nicholson doesn't look like a blacksmith!" Well, he does, and he doesn't. He isn't the blacksmith whose smithy stands under the spreading chestnut tree, but what blacksmith is? Not all smiths are brawny, nor do they all have arms like iron bands. Some who specialize in ornamental ironwork look as aesthetic as any other artist, even Jack Nicholson.

*For example, Cary Grant in Clifford Odets's film of Llewellyn's *None but the Lonely Heart.*

The point is that this particular blacksmith will look and act as he would if Jack Nicholson had chosen to be a blacksmith instead of an actor, and he would be no less real than would Longfellow's stereotype. Nicholson would have to place himself in the time and the environment called for in the story. He would have to consider the smith's social status in that environment, his level of education, his racial and/or religious background, and so on, just as he would in setting up any other character.

Physically he would have to accustom himself to the use of strange tools (just as Clift had to adjust his reaction to a strange bedroom door), which he would accomplish by practice, but he would manipulate those implements in his own way, depending on his own skeletal and muscular makeup rather than on one belonging to an imaginary, stereotypical smith. Nicholson, for instance, might have to use more shoulder and body leverage in wielding a heavy hammer with arm strength alone. The difference would make Nicholson no less a blacksmith, only a less massive one.

However, learning to do something new is not as difficult as breaking and relearning a habit. For characteristics that have more to do with personality than with tricks of the trade, Nicholson would probably depend on the same mocking eyes, the same gently sneering grin, the same casual walk, and the same general hand movements, whether scratching his head or his stomach, that he uses in all of his characterizations. And he would still create a legitimate blacksmith, unique but real, as every blacksmith is, but, because he is Jack Nicholson, probably a good deal more interesting. Yet it is exactly because this particular blacksmith is someone unusual tha we are telling his story. So here, too, Nicholson fills the bill without distortion.

Beyond all this another element is at work. Most people are basically xenophobic—every stranger is a threat—but because our blacksmith, even though a new and different character, has certain recognizable and familiar traits (courtesy of Jack Nicholson), he is more readily accepted by the viewer. The elimination of distrust permits quicker self-identification and deeper involvement in the film.

An in-depth study of a role will occasionally expose an invalid contradiction or a dramatically unprofitable character. A change will be in order. An apt example is the character of Christian

Diestl, as played by Marlon Brando in *The Young Lions*. At the time the film was made, there was a good deal of controversy and debate about the reason for, the incentive toward, and the result of the change in the character—Almost all of it based on rumor and unfounded statements. Only the screen writer, Edward Anhalt, and Marlon Brando and I were responsible for character alteration, and only we three know exactly what happened and why.

Irwin Shaw's exceptional novel was written immediately after World War II at a time when people's emotions concerning that holocaust were till near high tide. Nazis were the brutal enemy, and all the Germans were Nazis and therefore brutal. One of the novel's three leading characters was Christian, a young German caught up in the ferment of his time. He starts out as an honest patriot searching, as many Germans were, for international respect. He believes in Hitler not as a Nazi but as a political messiah, and he discounts reported atrocities as temporary aberrations that will soon be eliminated. With the start of the war he becomes a soldier and, as the war progresses, his personality is brutalized until at the end, he is transformed into a completely amoral, destructive human being. In short, he demonstrates that Nazism is a debasing philosophy.

The trouble was that when the film was made, some ten years later, every one knew that, and to say it again served no new purpose. Besides, by that time we also knew that millions of good Germans had opposed Hitler and had been executed for their pains.

In translating the novel to the screen we found no problems with the two American roles, but we felt that Christian's character left us nowhere to go but down and, in light of the public's current (1957) attitudes, gave us no opportunity to make fresh comments about Nazism or the effects of the war. In a truly communal effort we decided such comments could be made more forcefully if we started out with a patriot who believes in the German effort to regain its national pride and its pre-World War I status, but who learns, as the war progresses, that the ends do not justify the means. (This is not a new idea but it can certainly bear frequent repeating.) Through Christian's eyes we see how the Nazi leadership brutalizes those who follow it blindly. As he becomes gradually more aware of the true state of things, he realizes that all of his early hopes have been denied and he grows to abhor the whole Nazi concept. At the end, he smashes his weapon to bits and deliberately walks into an American soldier's bullet.

The evils of the Nazi movement were not overlooked; only against such a background could Christian's disillusionment be dramatized. But we felt that showing a German's realization of the corruption of the philosophy he once believed in would expose its weaknesses more effectively than if we saw it through the eyes of one of its enemies, which would, in a way, be begging the question.

Shaw, of course, disapproved of the changes. However, at least three out of four critics and viewers agreed with our point of view. Incidentally, the film was a tremendous success.

Those who objected to the change charged that Brando, unwilling to play an evil character, was responsible, a charge that was completely baseless. Brando was a cocontributor, nothing more. He has proved, both before and since our film, that playing "bad" characters is not one of his hang-ups.

The point here is that characters can be, and often are, changed to the benefit of the film. But they must always be real and, particularly in tragic drama, they must show growth or evolution. Otherwise, both the character and the story are literally flat. Whether the character is "good" or "bad," the viewer must find him interesting and, whether or not he agrees with his outlook on behavior, he must understand him.

Every student of human behavior knows that no man, however wicked he appears to society, thinks of himself as evil. He rationalizes his covert thoughts and his overt actions. He has a "good" reason for his behavior. For instance, I once asked a prisoner who was serving time for drug dealing if he had learned his lesson. I hoped, I said naively, that he would not continue in such a despicable trade when he was back in the streets.

"Despicable!" he said, with a show of astonishment. "Have you ever seen an addict who badly needs a fix? He suffers terrible pain. I am a benefactor, a doctor; I ease his pain and make his life more bearable."

The point was also made, less dramatically but with wider application, in *The Godfather*. One of the mobsters (it may have been the godfather himself) justifies his participation in bootlegging with, "I deal in services. If people didn't want what I sell I wouldn't be in business."

The creative actor must keep this concept in mind. In order to keep his character honest and not just an illustration, he must be able to rationalize all that character's behavior. He can also make the character more understandable, more appealing, let us say, by exhibiting some of the traits shared by most human beings. Again, in *The Godfather*, the title character is a strong family man—he loves his wife, his children, his grandchildren. He is faithful to his friends. He has an affinity for flowers. He loves dogs. He even loves his country, though he rationalizes the breaking of some of its laws, as do we all. (A prison warden once commented that if every citizen was held responsible for his legal transgressions practically every American would be in jail.) An actor who understands this will rarely say, "I can't play this man that way; I wouldn't do what he does." Of course he can, if he can find the proper rationalization. If it can't be found, either the actor is at fault or the character is dishonest, in which case it should be reconstructed.

It often becomes necessary for an actor to portray personally distasteful behavior, but the bases for nearly all behavior are present in most of us, and a simple extension of those bases can help the actor to make the necessary adjustments. For instance, an actor might say, "I can't play a murderer; I could never kill." Nonsense. Has he ever swatted a fly, squashed a spider, or stepped on an ant? They are all forms of life, and if he can take it at that level, he can kill—period. The adjustment is simple; he need only think of his victim as a gnat or (if he is a gardener) as a gopher or a snail. The substitution will furnish the motive for his behavior and will serve to settle him into any possible character, as long as that character is a valid example of humankind.

*   *   *

The actress speaks:

Putting yourself into a part you are given is what is expected. In About Face, *one of the leading characters was written as a scatter-brained, giggly girl who liked and went after the leading man. As if these characteristics weren't bad enough, she also had been given a lisp. The lines were written in this fashion:*

GIRL

Come on, thweetie. Leths have thom fun.
Leths danth!

Can you decipher, "Come on, sweetie. Let's have some fun. Let's dance!"?

When I was tested for the part, I had been given just one scene, and thought it a challenge. After getting the part, which ran all through the picture, I had a lot of work to do. After translating the lines, I practiced my own lisping night and day. I had to make this character easy and likable instead of obnoxious. When she popped up unexpectedly in the most unlikely places (like Bugs Bunny), I wanted the audience happy to see her, even if the character played by the leading man was not. The audience had to sympathize with her desire to be with this guy and with her efforts to get him. I was able to master the lisp to the point where I could ignore it mythelf, and all of my expressions and actions took over. She ended up being a truly pleasant and likable character and the director, Kurt Neuman, was very pleased. Hal Roach studio signed me to a long-term contract because of the response to this part.

When I heard that M.G.M. was looking for a teenage comedienne to play opposite Virginia Weidler in The Youngest Profession, *I wanted the part. The story was about two moviestar-crazy kids living in New York who would go to any and all lengths to get autographs of stars when they came to the city.*

My agent arranged an appointment with the director, and somehow he was able to get a script to me before the interview. The part was described as "a roly-poly comic, always falling down." Well, what could I do with that? It was a very good part, second lead, ran all the way through the film, and had scenes (cameos) with many of the top M.G.M. stars—William Powell, Greer Garson, Walter Pidgeon, Lana Turner, Hedy Lamarr—I had to have it.

After going over and over her scenes, I went in to the interview prepared to change the director's mind, convinced that I could make it better. My suggestion was that this character be played as a soft little girl with a Southern accent, absolutely overwhelmed whenever she is anywhere near a star. Instead of falling all over herself, she becomes almost immobile, mesmerized with awe. I read for him, sold him on my ideas, and got the job. The director, Edward Buzzell, encouraged me constantly and called me his protégé. After the film was finished I was awarded a long-term contract with Metro.

In Cry Danger I again played the second lead, a prostitute-pickpocket. I loved doing that part. We were able to make her so lovable that the audience felt broken-hearted when she was killed.

I've played myself many times in college musicals, singing and dancing and having a good time. No challenge there. It's easy for you when you're cast in a straight part. But even then, do everything you can to give some depth to the scenes. The main thing is to keep the audience's attention and make each person out there feel something for your character.

You can look at a bunch of lines, and read the story and understand it, but taking your character and bringing it to life, literally giving it life, that has to be you.

Imagine a character at the bottom of some stairs, looking up, then starting to climb. Is he a menacing villain? Or is she frightened of what's up there? Or is she being followed? Is it a character bringing home bad news, dreading the next few minutes? Or is this a girl filled with joy, having just left her lover, and is the audience aware that some kind of evil awaits her? See how many characters we can play? And each one of us would play it differently. As we should!

Can you imagine Debra Winger in the role Cissy Spacek played in Missing? They are both called "natural" actresses, and sometimes each comes off a little too natural. In trying to act natural, one has to be careful not to kick the dust.

And can you imagine Tom Courtney's version of Dustin Hoffman's Tootsie? Or Dustin Hoffman doing Paul Newman's role in Verdict? They're all fine actors, and each brings his own character and personality into a role.

Let me repeat here: don't ever go after a part unless you know you're right for it. I've heard actors say, "A good actor, a really fine actor, can play any part." Not true. Certainly not on the screen. In the theater, as a performance, possibly, but for the screen you must look the part. A cutie-pie, sexy actress would never be considered for the same roles given to Ingrid Bergman or Faye Dunaway or Meryl Streep, even if she were capable as an actress. Neither would the director cast any of those three names in a cutie-pie, sexy role. You see what I mean.

Try not to get yourself typed. You can't change certain physical things about yourself, but you can given them dimension and meaning. You will eventually find one certain thing about yourself that gets you the jobs. Latch on to it and use it.

Comedy is always a magic formula. Abbott and Costello in Hollywood *with Jean Porter and Frances Rafferty.*

8

The Magic Formula

Every filmmaker who has talked with groups of students has heard the question, "How do you do what you do? What is the formula?" So far as the question concerns the creative aspect of the enterprise, whether it be filmmaking or real estate development, the only honest answer is, "I don't know." A good deal can be taught, more can be learned, but you can't teach or learn talent. There is a formula, however, that is apropos.

Thomas A. Edison once wrote that genius is 1 percent inspiration and 99 percent perspiration. Using a common mathematical technique, let us substitute the word "talent" for the word "genius." Then 99 percent perspiration plus 1 percent inspiration equals talent. But that still leaves us short of a definitive answer, since that 1 percent often outweighs the value of the 99. At a more routine level, however, 99 percent P + 1 percent I = x can be translated as 99 percent preparation plus 1 percent implementation equals competence.

Good acting calls for a great deal of preparation, not only for each separate performance but for overall mastery of the craft. Every student of acting knows that career preparation involves thousands of hours, dozens of months, and many years of exercises. But acting exercises do not make the actor any more than writing exercises makes the novelist or practice in brush techniques makes a painter. If they did, we would have thousands of great writers, painters, athletes, and Oliviers. Exercise and practice, however, particularly practice, do help an artist to perfect his craft and to hone his talent, if he has any, for talent is inborn, and it comes in different sizes. The word "gift" is a synonym for "talent," and a most appropriate one, since talent is a gift, whether genetic or God-given. Without it, all the exercise and practice in the world will produce only a technician, a journeyman practitioner of any art.

A person possessing a gift is not always aware of it, often it is never given an opportunity to surface. But when it does it is, as a rule, recognized at once. For instance, it has long been known that mathematical genius shows itself at an early age, usually long before the start of any advanced training. The same is true for prodigies in music, painting, dancing, and so on. As for actors, one has only to note the number of startlingly good performances by children who have had no training at all. On the other side of the ledger are thousands of men and women who, driven by an irrepressible desire, have studied, exercised, and practiced all their working lives without developing anything beyond the most routine acting abilities. More than a few of these have polished their technical skills to the point where they can convince an uncritical viewer, but when their work is compared to that of a born actor, the difference is as obvious as that between a diamond and a rhinestone.

Whether one is gifted or a plodder, what are the exercises that can effectively perfect an actor's ability? In my opinion, the most important exercise by far is observation. An actor must be able to create a wide variety of characters, with an accompanying variety of intelligence and personality. For instance, Maximillian Schell, one of the finest of contemporary actors, played a Nazi officer in one film and a guilt-ridden Jew in another. In two other instances, the role of a musical genius was immediately followed by that of a mentally retarded saint. These four extremely divergent types, each possessing a unique personality and a different level of intelligence, were squeezed out of one intellect—his. But if he had not carefully observed these differing types as he had known them through his own experiences (with the possible exception of the saint), he could not have portrayed them so brilliantly on the screen.

An anecdote may help to drive home the concept. Schell was introduced to English-speaking audiences in my film *The Young*

Lions, in which he played a captain in Hitler's army. In his next film, *Judgment at Nuremberg*, he won the Oscar for playing a German lawyer defending Nazi officers against war-crime charges. On coming into a studio theater to see a preview of *The Reluctant Saint*, the wife of our publicity director remarked to her husband, "I'm not going to like this film. Schell is completely miscast. He can only play himself—an arrogant teutonic type." After the film, in which Max, as previously mentioned, played an "idiot" saint, she came up to me and apologized. "Schell is not only an actor," she said, "but a great actor. I am now completely convinced that he can play anything."

Of course, Schell did not play a saint. He played an apparently retarded young man whose basic goodness and simplicity enabled him to perform miracles, which, more than a hundred years later, resulted in his canonization. He learned how such a character might behave through observation of similar real human beings in their own environment, observations that he sharpened and dramatized through his own great talent.

Observation is preparation. One hour spent in observing people (or animals) in their environment is worth a month of technical exercises. And, the key to productive observation is the ability to penetrate those environments, no matter how alien they may be, without disturbing them unduly.

Nearly fifty years ago I read a book written by a well-known British biologist.* It concerned the study of the wild life in a West African jungle. In keeping with the principle of indeterminance, such a study is made difficult by the intrusion of the observer, since his presence immediately alters the environment. Sanderson's problem was to insert himself into the habitat without excessively upsetting it. He eventually realized that in the jungle, "Everything drifts slowly hither and thither as if wafted forward by currents and cross-currents. To stand still is to arouse suspicion. . . . I drifted and eddied with the animals themselves." He came upon a herd of wild river hogs: "Having drifted right in among them . . . I soon found myself right in the centre of the herd, noticed but unfeared by them."

Moving with the flow is not always easy. Some environments are difficult to penetrate, others are unfeasible. Walking into a

Animal Treasure by Ivan T. Sanderson. New York: Viking Press, 1937.

truck stop in a three-piece suit will get you no answers, nor will barging into a DAR convention in a punk rock outfit. Psychologists have long known that questioning a criminal, for instance, or a psychotic will elicit only the behavior and the answers that person believes you want to see and hear. To understand how a criminal really functions you have to infiltrate his way of life and, short of incurring a six-month prison sentence, that takes some doing. Even the great majority of criminal psychologists admit to only minimal success.

Lack of thorough understanding, whether of criminals or of any of a number of off-beat types, leads to stereotyping. The chief reason that so many dramatic portrayals are cliché is that the portrayer (and the writer) know only the stereotype. Once in a great while we see a character who is not stereotypical because the actor has taken the time and the trouble to get into his character's life. Such a portrayal is always highly effective, its truth is immediately apparent.

There is a world of difference between what seems true and what is true. As a boy of six in British Columbia I had a revelatory experience. We lived in a wild, mountainous region—rattlesnake country. While walking across a field one day I was startled by a sharp rattling sound. I stopped in my tracks and listened carefully. I thought I had heard a snake's rattle, but I wasn't quite sure. (Later, I determined that the sound was caused by a moving chain in an abandoned well.) Much more alert now, I moved on. A few minutes later I was again startled by a sharp rattle, but this time there was no doubt, no need to stop and listen. The hair on the back of my neck told me it was indeed the rattle of a snake.

An honest portrayal is like that—you just drink in the truth. There is no need, indeed, no desire, for critical evaluation. You simply "live" the vicarious experience.

But back to nuts and bolts. If you want to understand truck drivers put yourself into their milieu. You need not try to be a truck driver (they would probably spot the deception at once), you need only to be accepted by them. You can dress like them, try to use their language, or better yet, just listen. A few visits to truck stop cafes (if you can stand the coffee) will shatter the stereotype and set you on the way to a more honest characterization.

Some such exercises are easy, some very difficult, but you must learn to take advantage of every opportunity. Are you going in for a flu shot, a cold treatment, or a physical? Study your doctor during every visit; you may someday have to play one. If you attend classes, study your instructor more closely than you do your lessons; your marks may drop but you will learn more. And go to gatherings—all kinds of gatherings. Watch how people behave in church, at an evangelical meeting, a political rally, or a sports spectacle.

Shortly after World War II, I had occasion for the first time in my adult life to visit and work in England. I am an avid sports fan and I attended every athletic contest that was conveniently available. I was immediately struck by an unanticipated phenomenon: English hockey fans very closely resembled American hockey fans, their reactions to the various facets of the sport were identical. The behavior of British boxing aficionados was the same as that of their American cousins; the same hat-wearing, cigar-chewing, bet-making types peopled both nations' fight arenas. The same was true for wrestling, tennis, track and field, even for soccer, which I paired off against our baseball.* But what shook me was that the British boxing fan resembled the British hockey fan far less than he resembled his American counterpart.**

The same observation is made by every filmmaker who visits a foreign studio, whether in London, Rome, or Bombay. Once on a sound stage, the filmmaker is at home. Even though the workers speak a different tongue, their movements, attitudes, even their surface appearances are strikingly similar.

The theory that members of a similar class from a variety of countries are much more akin than are members of different classes of the same nationality was not new to me, but the startling testimony to its validity was a revelation. So here, too, is one more source of character delineation—class distinction.

There are a number of ways to get the feel of an unfamiliar class. One is to surround yourself with some of its accoutrements

---

*The only sport for which I could find no parallel was cricket, which is like no other sport on earth.

**I later found the same similarities and differences existing in France, Italy, and other countries.

during your period of preparation. In a novel written a century ago by J. K. Huysmans, the chief character is an avidly curious but spiritually depleted Frenchman who finds it difficult to stray from his familiar surroundings. Wishing to visit the London of Dickens, he satisfies his desire in a most unusual way.

He packs his trunk and starts off for the railroad station, but first stops at a book mart to buy an English travel guide. He browses through a number of them, reading about the London Museum with its paintings by familiar artists—following a Baedecker guidebook *of Paris*—he visits an English wine shop where he savors a glass of port and observes the convivial Britishers at play. His next stop is an English restaurant. Here he finds himself in the midst of more British types. Ordering oxtail soup, smoked haddock, roast beef and boiled potatoes, and some Stilton cheese, he dines with relish, washing the meal down with a couple of pints of ale. Leaving the restaurant, he retrieves his trunk and returns home, satisfied that he has experienced the best of London without ever leaving Paris.

Perhaps a touch bizarre, or just plain crazy, but it does carry the seed of an idea. You, too, can surround yourself with the trappings of your character's class. Small furnishings, books, magazines, selected sports paraphernalia, and the like should not be too expensive or difficult to acquire. Visit his special haunts and eat his special foods, and try to enjoy them. Such an immersion into your character's life will bring more than a touch of reality into your characterization.

Maurice Chevalier once described another technique for thinking yourself into a role, one he practiced as a young man. Standing before a mirror, he thought of himself as alienated from society, homeless, starving—a street beggar looked back at him from the glass. In this manner he ran successfully through a number of sharply differentiated characters, but then found himself in trouble—he essayed the role of a churchman. He thought of himself as adoring God, full of holiness, selflessness, faith, and charity. The face staring back at him was completely unfamiliar. So, taking a different tack, he thought of himself as ambitious, greedy, self-indulgent, full of cupidity, and with a lust for power. Voila! The mirror reflected the face of a classic career bishop. (This is Chevalier's story, not mine.)

Another area that will repay serious study is the field of aptitude testing, which relies more on a person's habits, inclinations, fancies, and tastes than it does on innate skills or IQ. If you are about to undertake the role of a surgeon, for instance, aptitude criteria will tell you what inclinations the best surgeons have in common. Knowing and resorting to such data whenever possible can help to bring about the realization of a desired character.

Books are a ubiquitous source of information. Any actor attempting to learn about a variety of personalities through experience alone will find himself still woefully unprepared at the end of his life. A great deal of what we know must be learned vicariously, and the experiences of those who are skilled at communicating their insights are certainly among the best and most prolific sources of human observation. The odds are that no actress about to play a prostitute would care to get the necessary experience at first hand. But a careful reading of Kuprin's *Yama (The Pit)* will give her as much information as would a year spent in a brothel.

However, when using second-hand experience, there is a caveat. Since even the most impartial of observers often make subjective judgments, it is wise to get at least a second opinion. Fortunately, a host of such opinions is as close as your nearest library.

Whether first-hand or vicarious, all these sources must be double-checked, tested, and weighed against each other, and finally sifted through your own ever-growing understanding of the human condition. Only then can you consider yourself a professional. And, whatever the level of excellence your talent allows you, if you are a true student of the art, you will become a better actor with each passing day.

*   *   *

The actress speaks:

Observation will make you a comedian, if you don't watch out. And what could be better? Knowing how to play comedy will get you anywhere.

Comedy is our most popular form of entertainment. Everyone likes to laugh, and more important, everyone likes to identify. Mr. and Ms. Average love to see something happening on the screen that has happened to them, where they have been laughed at or have laughed at themselves; or better yet, something they might have thought of but didn't dare do.

You don't have to be a clown to be funny. The best comedy comes out of natural, everyday living, and concerns things with which all persons can identify, simple things.

Observe a woman in a supermarket, standing at some distance, watching a man who is troubled with the tedious job of choosing which prepared dinners to take home from the frozen food counter. Aha! Obviously, he's a bachelor, and you can check her basket contents and see that she is single. This is a comedy situation that any actor would like to play. If you've never experienced it, rush out to your nearest supermarket, take a basket, pick out a few things, and park near the frozen dinners. Watch the men, then watch the women who watch the men. Most rewarding.

There are other places for encountering natural comedy situations. In a large, busy drugstore there is usually a seat near the pharmaceutical center where the elderly wait for their prescriptions. Here you can pick up an abundance of material by watching and listening. And, of course, in restaurants and bars.

Another place to study human behavior is the Social Security welfare office. Here you can sit among the people in the waiting room and pick up conversations, then wander closer to where you can overhear interviews. This will enlighten you in many areas and show you parts of life that can only be called tragicomic. Skid Row in L.A. or the down-trodden area of any big city is another place, as is the inside of a mental institution or the Motor Vehicles Department.

You may be saying, "But this is writing material, creating stuff . . ." True, it can be. But what it is is studying people in their natural environment. Make notes, mental and written, and file them away for future reference. One day you may need to recall these experiences as a suggestion, or an accompaniment to a part you're given. It all helps you to be prepared when called for the different categories and variations of roles. To be creative, especially in comedy, you have to have seen, if not experienced, the humor behind all this seriousness. Real humor most often comes from trying to resolve a serious situation (see any Laurel and Hardy comedy).

To study situation comedy, watch Cary Grant and Irene Dunn in The Awful Truth and My Favorite Wife, and William Powell and Myrna Loy in The Thin Man. Sure, they were given great material, excellent direction and editing, but these actors pulled it off. They are given the credit for some of the best comedies ever put on film.

Blatant and over-obvious comedy may be good for a chuckle, but it certainly doesn't touch the heart. And, more often than not, it's called crude and vulgar, especially if blended with foul language. This offends many people and ruins many an intended effect.

Good, natural, funny situations with actors who understand timing and reaction—this is what it's all about.

Final touch-ups are given to Jean Porter before shooting a musical number in Little Miss Broadway.

9

Help Is on the Way!

On the sound stage an actor is never on his own. Whether he likes it or not, he is always surrounded by "helpers." These helpers exercise certain controls that he occasionally resents, but they also make available certain opportunities that while curbing self-indulgence, make it possible for him to give a performance of greater depth and impact than he could in any other medium.

The controls, of course, are the fly in the actor's soup. Most actors, at one time or another, have complained that the director and the cutter are really responsible for their performances since it is they who control the editing process. A partial motivation for this complaint is the fear that the actor may wind up as "the face on the cutting room floor." But the true intent of any director or cutter I have ever known has been to present each actor's efforts in the best interest of the film, and if the film benefits, so does the actor. Such aims involve questions of judgment and are subject to error. In the majority of cases, however, an actor's performance is rarely damaged in the editing process; it is more often enhanced. But long before postproduction comes into play, the total impact of an actor's work can be expanded in a number of ways.

An actor entering the film field should acquire the best possible understanding of who his helpers are and of the nature of their assistance. But, first, let us examine how actors with an inclination toward self-indulgence can be circumvented.

Do you insist on doing it "your way"?

Many years ago a budding actress (who later became one of the screen's great talents) disagreed with her director (later equally renowned) about the way a certain scene should be played. Discussion failed to bring agreement, persuasion had no power. The actress insisted on doing her thing. Without further argument the director surrendered to her demands, doing the same scene take after take after take, hour after hour after hour. Finally, about midnight, the actress decided to try the director's version. "cut," said the director, after the shot. "Print it, and let's all go home!"

Do you insist on having the "topper"?

The on-set confrontations of two well-known sophisticated comedy stars were well known. Each would try to "top" the other, and each had his or her own gag writer on the set. When Charlie Ruggles surprised Mary Boland with a punch line in the first take (which he frequently did), she, after a quick conference with her gag man, would top him in the second. The see-sawing could go on for hours, and often did. I was cutting one of their films and remarked upon the amusing but frustrating situation to Leo McCarey, the director, more in sympathy than in any hope of a solution. "Oh, I don't let it bother me," he said. "It keeps them on their toes. And I know you have a very sharp pair of scissors."

Do you insist on dominating the scene?

The scissors are the answer to a number of selfish tricks. In one of my films a method actor was eternalizing an "internalization." As staged, he is seated in a chair with his back to the camera. Immediately after the start of the scene he rises, turns, and walks toward the camera, which pans him into a two-shot for the continuation of the take. The actor insisted that he remain seated for an interminable length of time (probably more than a minute) while he internalized his emotions before rising and continuing with the scene. He thought it would play. Without any argument, I prepared to roll. The cameraman thought I was losing control. Somewhat startled, he whispered, "Eddie, you can't use that pause! It's a dreadful stall!" I nodded, then moved the index and middle fingers of my hand in imitaion of snipping scissors. He suddenly smiled. For the moment he had forgotten that I was in control of the only control that really counted— the control afforded by a small pair of scissors.

Do you insist on hogging the camera?

Directors also control the camera set-ups. Actors are human beings and a few of them, as such, may be selfish. Some will make stabs at upstaging their fellow actors before they learn the futility of such attempts, and slow learners must occasionally be taught a lesson. A bright, talented, but self-centered young actress in one of my films illustrated the point. She had not been around long enough to realize that upstaging in a properly made film is impossible, since there is no up or down stage on a film set. Through the courtesy of a mobile camera, the viewer has a 360-degree point of view. When the actress, pleading inexperience in hitting her marks, persisted in trying to hog the camera, I simply flipped it around into a close-up of her coplayer, eliminating her altogether. When I did not shoot a complementary close-up of her, she realized that her attempts at hogging the camera would only present her fellow artist with a large close-up every time she tried to upstage her. Being, in reality, a quick study, she never tried it again.

It is a mistake for the actor to try to maneuver himself into what he sees as the most advantageous position with respect to the camera. That is one of the functions of the director, and a good director will use his camera more to enhance the actor's performance than as a means of chastisement. His set-ups will be contrived to most effectively present the actor's reactions and movements in any particular part of the scene, subject always, however, to the relative importance of every other actor in that scene. When more than one performer occupies the frame, the actor must realize that he may not always be the essential center of interest, and that the purposes of the scene may best be served only by what he may consider preferential treatment of another player. But if the film benefits, so does he. It is far better to be a solid contributor in a fine film than a big star in a stinker. And always remember, the actor who consistently has his back to the camera in the full shots may wind up with the majority of close-ups in the edited film.

Besides helping the actor by presenting him to the viewer in the most effective shots at the most effective times, the director also carefully selects the lenses with which those shots are made. A 50mm lens, for instance, will shot the actor as seen by the naked eye (modified only by the quantity and quality of makeup that may be used). But if I want to impart a more menacing appearance to a character, I do not ask the actor to "act" the extra menace. That would probably be unreasonable as far as the character is concerned, and possibly quite hammy as far as the acting is concerned. I would simply shoot the scene with a wide-angle lens, which distorts the features, and with a little help in "menace lighting" from the cameraman, I would obtain a visual effect of menace while leaving the actor at liberty to give a natural, honest, performance, free of any distortion of the basic character. If, on the other hand, I want to add an extra dimension of beauty to the leading lady's close-up, I would shoot her with a narrow-angle lens (75 or 100mm), which serves to ameliorate any undesirable natural distortions in her features (such as a slightly too-long nose). By diminishing the depth of focus, the same lens permits me to zero in on her eyes while putting her ears and the tip of her somewhat shortened nose slightly out of focus.

The role of an expert boxer in a classic film was played by an exceptionally good actor, but there was a problem. The exceptionally good actor couldn't throw a good straight punch. In the long shots, a fighting double could, and did, fit the bill. But a large number of close shots are always needed, especially when, as in this instance, the fight is a vital part of the climax. How can you make an actor who throws a punch like a girl look like a champion? Don't try to guess. In this instance it was managed by reversing the action. In other words, the actor extended his arm, his shoulder, and his body as far as he could toward the camera. Then, with all the speed and energy at his command (aided by an undercranked camera) he drew his arm and shoulder back as far as he could. When the film was printed in reverse the effect was that of a beautiful straight jab, delivered with speed and power—another prime example of the screen's "magic"—a magic available in no other medium.

The manipulation of camera speed, as used to facilitate the shooting of fight scenes, is applicable in many other situations. Added speed is supplied by wide-angle lenses and/or underspeeding the camera. An interesting series of diverse effects can be manufactured through the use of slow motion (now often a cliché, but still effective when creatively used). Slow motion can add grace and ease to an actor's movements, or it can make them appear to be labored and difficult to effect. A wide-angle lens, head on, can make an actor walking normally seem to be taking giant strides, while a telescopic lens shooting the same action will show him to be struggling to take steps that appear to be only a few inches long.

By the use of lighting and filters, the cameraman can enhance the actor's appearance. (Such techniques are used not only for women.) Proper shadowing can add beauty and character to a "normal" face. Cross-lighting will accentuate lines and wrinkles, aging an actor a number of years without resorting to excessive use of makeup, whereas flat lighting can remove those same lines and make the face appear to be more youthful than it is in reality. And a properly used eyelight will add life and vitality to an actor's expression—a most desirable quality in any characterization.

The careers of many actors of both sexes have been considerably extended through the use of lens filters to disguise or obliterate the normal scars of time or disease. "Portrait" lighting enabled one well-known actress to sustain a reputation for beauty throughout a long career even though her face carried the scars of a childhood bout with small-pox.

The final aid comes in the cutting room, where the selection of the best portions of the various shots are made for the final assembly. Given enough time and takes on the set, an actor can always deliver a "perfect" performance, at least as far as his talent allows perfection. Here, too, pace can be corrected or altered to any desired degree, inadequate performances ameliorated, and dramatic action, or reaction, highlighted.*

In the final stages of postproduction, sound manipulation can, when necessary, work small wonders with the actors' voices, and the addition of musical underscoring can add mood and emphasis to their performances. (This is most effectively demonstrated in sequences of suspense.)

All this may cause the budding actor to say, "But where is the fun or the creative satisfaction in all this? Everything is being done for me!" Well, not quite. Experienced actors have learned that they can more easily concentrate on portraying real, honest

---

*See Dmytryk *On Film Editing*. Boston: Focal Press, 1984.

human beings when they are freed from the necessity of creating excessively dramatic performances. (Spencer Tracy could play "Mr. Hyde" with an absolute minimum of the gruesome makeup traditionally used and, in the process, come much closer to a believable interpretation of Stevenson's tale.)*

The actor can still shout when shouting is called for, gesticulate wildly when the occasion demands, or make a face when it is justified by the situation. But he need go no further in any of these directions than would his character in real life. Any excesses in appearance or activity needed for dramatic emphasis can and will be supplied by his helpers. (Though, for his own good, he'd better not call them that!)

*   *   *

The actress speaks:

Once you have been given a part you have the whole company, the whole studio, behind you, rooting for you, so to speak. They are all there to help you look and sound your best. All you have to do is be as good as they believe you are.

Do you practice acting for the screen? Do you attend special screen-acting classes?

When I taught film acting in Austin, Texas, I wrote some special one-person scenes for some of my actors. With video equipment, we recorded them on tape. The tapes were invaluable in analyzing the exercises and later helped them in getting jobs.

I'm going to give you some of these scenes, right here, for you to use as exercises, if you care to. The camera is on you at all times, and there are no other voices. You must assume the other person is opposite you, just off camera or on the other end of the phone, and you listen to his (or her) words. Please remember all that has been said about the importance of listening on camera. The camera (audience) is taking in all the other person is saying by watching you and your reactions. Keep the pace, but don't rush it. Get it just right.

---

*More complete descriptions of the techniques mentioned in this chapter can be obtained from Dmytryk, *On Screen Directing,* and Dmytryk, *On Film Editing.* Boston: Focal Press, 1984.

SCENE I

THE OBSCENE TELEPHONE CALL

> The scene opens with SANDY, a young girl in her early twenties, looking through a public telephone book. She can be in bed or lounging on a couch. Flipping the pages, she sees a name she likes, puts her finger on it, then runs it across the page to the number. She looks at it carefully then, on the push-button phone near her, she punches out the seven digits and waits for an answer. (While the phone is ringing on the other end, show your anticipation—mildly, don't overdo it—for what's ahead.) As a voice comes into her ear, you react, then speak.

SANDY

Hello, this is an obscene telephone call.
(pause)
You like it?

She pauses while a man speaks.

SANDY (cont.)

Well . . . I mean . . . do you like . . . do you like the obscene telephone call?
(pause, listening)
Well, it's gonna get better.
(pause)
Ah . . . well, ah . . . don't go away. Are you interested?
(pause, listening)
You're interested. . . . Ah . . . how would you like it? I mean, ah, how obscene would you like it?
(pauses, listening)
You'd like it very obscene. Uh . . . have you ever received an obscene telephone call before?
(pause)

SANDY (cont.) You haven't?
. . . But you've always wanted to? . . . Hm. . . . Right!
(pause)

(continued)

I (continued)

> Yes. No! . . . no, no. No, I'm not going to give
> you my name.
>> (rattled)
> Of course I'm not going to give you my name.
> This is an obscene phone call . . . you think
> I'm going to give you my name?!
>> (pause)
> You're right! I haven't done this before. No, I
> haven't.
>> (pause)
> No. I'm not going to give you my name. . . .
> You want to give me your name? Oh, I know
> your name. I got it from the phone book.
>> (laughs)
> Sidney. Sidney likes obscene phone calls.
>> (pause)
> No, I don't know. . . . No, you don't know me.
>> (pause)
> No. I just decided to do this.
>> (pause)
> Yeah . . . this is really kind of interesting,
> because you don't know who you're talking
> to. . . . You'll never know me. I can say
> anything I want to you.
>> (pause)
> I will. I . . . can say anything I want to you.
>> (pause)
> I will. I . . . I made up my mind that I
> was. . . . WHAT?!
>> (pause)
> What did you say?

There is a long pause while Sandy actually turns red in the face.

> SANDY (cont.)
> WWHAAT?! . . . How dare you!

She pauses in shock and embarrassment.

(continued)

I (continued)

> SANDY (cont.)
> How dare you say such a thing to me, because
> I know who you are. You are a terrible,
> terrible person. And don't you ever, ever speak
> to me that way again! Don't you ever dare call
> me again!

Sandy abruptly hangs up the phone and looks directly into the camera, realizing what she has done.

Played for comedy, of course, this scene can end in at least two ways. I had Sandy look into the camera, deadpan, a little surprised, still digesting the outcome of something she had planned entirely differently.

Eddie directed this scene and had her finish it by looking into the camera with a mischievous smile, as though she had baited the guy into saying things she wanted to hear. (If you want to milk the laughs, you can finish off by having her look back into the phone book for another number.)

Take your choice, kids.

SCENE II

GOODBYE, DARLING

> The scene opens on VIRGINIA, a middle-aged lady (sixtyish)
> greying hair, beautifully styled, dressed in the best of taste. She
> leans against the wall, just outside a hospital room. She has been
> sniffling into a handkerchief and we see the grief in her face as
> she looks toward a nurse who has just walked up and who now
> speaks from OFF-SCREEN. (VOICE OVER)

*(Note: This is the only line that will be a VOICE OVER. It
introduces the scene.)*

> NURSE'S VOICE (O.S.)
> Mrs. Kershaw, we've done everything possible
> to save your husband, but he won't make it
> through the night. The doctor says you may
> have a few moments alone with him, if you
> wish.
>
> VIRGINIA
> (speaking to the nurse)
> Is he aware? Will he know I am there?

> No answer from the nurse is necessary. Virginia gives a weak
> and kindly nod of understanding. She then dabs her nose, pulls
> herself together, and goes through the door.

*(Note: This is easy video camera work. Simply pan her inside
the hospital room and go with her a very short distance as she
approaches what is supposed to be a hospital bed. You can use
a long table, with white sheets simulating a body. In camera
view, show barely the top of the sheet, thus enabling us to believe
the actress is speaking to her dying husband.)*

> Inside the hospital room Virginia closes the door behind her and
> walks up to the single bed in the room. She appears to be looking
> directly into her husband's face, and the audience is allowed to
> wonder about her thoughts. She speaks softly to him, and reaches
> out to touch him.

(continued)

II (continued)

                    VIRGINIA
Howard . . ? Howard, can you hear me?

A pause, then she reacts to his opening eyes . . . his look to her.
She speaks softly and sweetly.

                    VIRGINIA (cont.)
Yes . . . yes, it is I. Your beloved wife of so
many years. . . . Oh, Howard . . . I think
back to our first years together . . . our
young years. The joy! The respect! The pure
unadulterated adoration I felt for you . . . the
naivete. . . . Oh, how young I was! Then I
grew up, didn't I? But you continued to treat
me as that same child . . . how sweet. . . .
But Howard, during those years I became wise
and inquisitive. . . . I guess you thought I
was as simple as ever, or that I didn't
care. . . . You never guessed that I watched
everything you did. . . . I watched as your
business grew from the losses of others. I
watched as you took on strength as others
failed. . . . You never trusted those who
should not have trusted you. . . . And our
children . . . you've never been able to
tolerate Elizabeth and Martin . . . but those
two idiots are yours! But Howard . . .
Howard, can you hear me. . . ?
                    (she looks carefully
                    and deeply into his eyes)
. . . Yes . . .
                    (a brief pause)
Howard . . . our son Robert, our brilliant son,
Robert, your adored son, Robert . . . is not
your son.
                    (a brief pause)
                    VIRGINIA (cont.)
Oh, yes, you've left everything to him. . . .
                    (a brief pause)
He's mine, but he is not yours.
                    (She pauses briefly,
                    watching his face)
Why, Howard . . . I haven't seen your eyes
opened that wide in years.
                                        (continued)

II (continued)
                              (a brief pause)
            Yes.
                         (changes tone, quietly)
            Our son Robert is not your son. Take that to
            your grave, you son-of-a-bitch!

She pauses, watches his face carefully as he expires.

                         VIRGINIA (cont.)
            Howard. . . ?

She reaches to feel his pulse, her eyes still watching his face
carefully. When she is satisfied that he is gone, she puts herself
back into the character of the bereaved widow, lifts her kerchief
to her nose, and CALLS OUT as she starts for the door.

                         VIRGINIA (cont.)
            Nurse!

She exits.

SCENE III

LATE

The scene opens as PAM, a beautiful young girl in her mid-twen-
ties, rushes breathlessly through a door, closes it behind her,
and leans against it. She looks straight ahead (just off CAMERA
LEFT) to an unseen man whom the audience will get to know
through her dialogue. (He will say just two words OFF CAMERA
to start the scene. No more.) PAM has been running and is
breathing heavily as we hear his VOICE OVER.

                         MAN (O.S.)
          You're late.

Still breathing hard, Pam continues looking directly at him. She
moves forward just an inch or two. With a rather smug look, she
reaches into her bag, takes out a scarf and displays within it—
a gun. After a couple of seconds she tosses it onto his desk (which
has been placed directly in front of where she is to stand, but
not necessarily showing on camera.

                            PAM
                   (still breathing hard)
          That was hardly an easy job you sent me on. I
          could have been a lot later. In fact . . . a hell
          of a lot later. . . .

She pauses, listens to him intently.

                        PAM (cont.)
          Trouble. . . ? Oh, just enough to make it
          interesting.
                     (pauses, listening)
          Mike, when he finds the gun missing, he'll
          know I took it.
                     (pauses, listening)
          No, I don't think I was followed.
                     (pauses, listening)
          I said think because I don't know! How does
          ̇one know? It's dark out there. I changed cabs
          twice, and I've been running.
                     (listens, watches him)
          Of course I was running. I was rushing to get

                                            (continued)

III (continued)

> here like you said. Look . . . I'm sure I wasn't
> followed, and you've got the gun. What do I
> get?

From off camera Mike pitches her a key which she grabs. She
looks at the metal tag on the key and laughs a sarcastic laugh.

> PAM (cont.)
> Bonanza King?! . . . What is this? A key to a
> hidden treasure? A free hamburger . . . ?
> What kind of a detective are you . . . ? I want
> to be paid!
> (pauses, listening)
> The key to your . . . ??? Mike, I'm new in
> this business, but I'm good. I know it's a
> short-lived business, but I also know that it
> pays well. I wanna be paid now . . . C.O.D., as
> promised.
> (a pause)
> Your place . . . ? Michael, I felt I was lucky
> enough to get here . . . and I just might make
> it to the airport.

During this last line she has opened her bag, pulled out her neat
little black gloves, and has put them on as she speaks. As she
finishes putting them on, she pauses.

> PAM (cont.)
> Once more. Pay now??

Pam looks steadily at Michael, then starts to shake her head as
though he has just said, "no."

> PAM (cont.)
> I've heard of the old double-cross. How do you
> like this one?

She reaches quickly into her bag and draws out another gun,
which she points directly at Michael.

> PAM (cont.)
> Your friend had a wad of dough on him, and
> two guns. . . . Now you'll have them
> both. . . .

(continued)

III (continued)

> (aiming carefully,
> ready to shoot)

No, no, Mike. . . . Too late.

BANG!!! she shoots. Then she tosses the second gun onto his desk, gives his body a cool glance, turns and walks out.

There are several very important things to remember about this scene. First is pace. She has been running, and though her heavy breathing can lessen as the scene progresses, she is still UP. Second, when it is decided (by whoever is directing this) where Michael is to sit, be certain that you look directly at him, into his eyes. If you have to use your imagination to conjure up this character, put him in one place and keep him there. The viewer must see your eyes, so the camera (if any) should be set low, shooting up slightly, and Michael's chair should be raised a bit so that your eyes look directly at him. The audience must see your eyes, and through them your feelings.

SCENE IV

NOT GUILTY

The placement of two off-camera characters is important to this scene. One is the judge to whom most of the scene is played. He should be very CLOSE CAMERA LEFT, and a little above eye level, as though he were up on the bench. The other is BARBARA'S husband, seated some distance to the judge's left, and below eye level. BARBARA looks to the judge as she speaks to him, then glances occasionally at, or to, her husband. This girl is neurotic.

The scene opens as BARBARA approaches the bench. (She will take one step into CENTER CAMERA, MEDIUM CLOSE, and look directly at the judge.)

                          BARBARA
          Please, Judge, let me speak for my husband.
          He isn't telling you the truth. I take the oath.
          He is not guilty.
                    (she pauses, listening)
          No, he was not at home with me . . . but I
          know he couldn't possibly be the person
          you're looking for . . .
                          (a pause)
          He's an honest man. . . .
                    (she looks at Jim,
                    her husband)
          Look at him . . . you can see it.
                    (back to Judge)
          He has no record of any previous
          violations. . . .
                    (pause, listening)
          Statement? . . . His statement admitting guilt
          is thoroughly and completely false. . . .
          That's why I'm here.
                    (pause, listening)
          Yes . . . yes, I believe he is protecting
          someone.
                    (pause, listens)
          I can't tell you that.
                          (pause)
                                        (continued)

IV (continued)

> Cannot? Will not? . . . What difference? I will
> not if I cannot.
>> (pause)
> I don't know.

Barbara looks to her husband for a couple of seconds, then back
to the Judge, and we see a change of pace.

>> BARBARA (cont.)
> Yes, I do know. . . . Her name is Franceska
> Borro . . . she lives at twenty-two eleven
> Oakridge Drive.

Another glance to her husband, then quickly back to the Judge.

>> BARBARA (cont.)
> You will find some of my husband's things
> there, but I'm sure you will also find proof
> that it was she who killed Mr. Lockhart.
>> (pause)
> Why didn't I tell you this before? Because I
> expected my husband to tell you . . . but of
> course . . . no . . .
>>> (a short glance to
>>> her husband and back)
> He is the martyr . . .
>> (nasty)
> The hero. He would die to protect his love.

She looks long at her husband and we see her start to break.
Tears start to form.

>> BARBARA (cont.)
> Oh, my God!
>> (tears)
> Oh, Jim, what have I done?

She snaps back to the Judge.

>> BARBARA (cont.)
> No! What I've told you is a lie. It was I! . . .
> Yes. Please believe me. I am the guilty one.
> He's protecting me!

She looks again to her husband.

(continued)

IV (continued)

                    BARBARA (cont.)
        Oh, Jim. . . .
                    (questioning)
        You did know. . . ?
                    (back to Judge)
        You see? He loves me. He is protecting me.

    She glances at her husband, then back to the Judge.

                    BARBARA (cont.)
                    (breathing hard)
        Oh, my God. . . .

I've been asked time and again to explain how to cry real tears. All it takes is experience and living—caring—heart. The feeling must be real, then the tears come easily. If you are playing a scene where you have just been told your best friend has been killed in an accident, the tears are not immediate. At first, the shock is one of disbelief. Then you have to think about it. Here is where the heart comes forth. You think of the last time you saw him, that you will never see him again, that you didn't know you would never see him again, the things unsaid. Dozens of thoughts such as these flash through your mind and if you really feel it, the tears will be there before you realize it.

You cannot manufacture tears. Oh, yes, if an actor simply cannot cry, the director will kindly suggest that he turns his head and pretend to weep, shoulders trembling, perhaps. Or you can cry into your hands. But you have to look up sometime! Directors and editors are masters at putting together a crying scene. They can always "cut to the kitchen stove" while a makeup person puts a liquid into the eyes of the heroine, then cut quickly into a close shot of her and, voila! BooHoo. But when you really feel a sad scene it isn't only the tears, it's everything that goes with it. Not long ago I watched a top actor in an Academy Award-winning film do a crying scene and never saw a tear or felt his sadness. He screamed his lines and grimaced to show his pain, but I felt nothing. 'Tis said he gave a good performance.

Laughter! How does one laugh on the screen! Well, for one thing, you certainly can't be in a sour mood. The scene, as written, must give you cause to laugh, but like a very tired, too-

often-repeated joke (after you've studied the script at length) it probably no longer seems funny to you. So, you laugh anyway. If you have studied singing and breath control you can manu-facture a laugh. If you don't sing, take a deep breath and let it out as you make laughing sounds (even ha,ha,ha works). Keep this going until you feel so silly you will actually be laughing at yourself. You can do it. Keep it up. Do the scale. Up and down. Start down and go up. Then start up and go down. It's fun! And don't worry about the neighbors as you practice. This is Hollywood.

SCENE V

BEST COFFEE IN TOWN

> A young man quickly steps into CENTER CAMERA (CLOSE) as
> though he has just darted out of the rain. (He is in the alcove
> of a store front.) He has been sheltering his head with a folded
> newspaper and he begins to shake the water from it and to brush
> himself off. Suddenly he looks directly at someone CAMERA
> RIGHT. A young woman has spoken to him (OFF CAMERA). We
> have not heard a word,

JEFF

Oh, yeah . . . wet . . .

> Jeff looks around at the street action, but is again attracted by
> her voice.

JEFF (cont.)

New here in L.A.? . . . Yeah. . . .
(wondering)
How could you tell?
(pause, listening)
My clothes? . . . They're just ordinary
clothes.
(pause, while she speaks)
Raincoat! Oh . . . don't the people here wear
raincoats?
(a pause)
Better things to spend their money on . . . I
suppose so . . .
(looks at her carefully)
You look cold.
(pause, then, a statement)
You're not.
(pause)
What? . . . A cup of coffee? . . . No, thanks.
(pause)

JEFF (cont.)

You'll pay? . . . That makes no difference to
me. . . . You'll pay! That would be absurd, as
a matter of fact.
(listening)

(continued)

V (continued)

> Vermillion. I'm from Vermillion, South
> Dakota.
>> (a pause)
> I am. . . . I am proud of it. A sweet place it is.
>> (thinking of it)
> Small and sweet.
>> (pauses, listening)
> What did you say? So my?? . . . Oh . . . so are
> you.
>> (looking her up
>> and down)
> So you are.
>> (a pause)
> No, I don't want to go for a cup of coffee. And
> listen, young lady, where I come from the
> man asks the woman.
>> (listens, frowns)
> It's not old fashioned! . . . It's . . . it's just
> the right way to do things.

Jeff watches her carefully. He feels he may have hurt her feelings.

>> JEFF (cont.)
> You're shivering. You are cold. . . . I'll give
> you my coat and take you for a cup of coffee.
>> (pause)
> No!! . . . Why not?
>> (pause)
> You'll . . . make me some coffee at your
> place? . . .
>> (thinks about it,
>> listening)
> Best coffee in town?
>> (pause)
> You know . . . I've heard of things like this
> happening. You're crazy. How do you know
> I'm not a dangerous criminal?
>> (watching her laughter)
> Well, you don't have to get hysterical . . .

He stares at her *(and here you have a choice of attitudes—a chance to swing it in one of several directions).*

(continued)

V (continued)

                              JEFF (cont.)
          Let's go.

     They exit.

SCENE VI

CAUGHT

     The scene opens with a young man standing with his back to
     the camera (which should be angled). He is going through a file
     drawer in an office filing cabinet. We feel his anxiety by his
     movements. He searches rather frantically. Suddenly, there is
     the SOUND of a door opening. Startled, he turns towards us,
     looking off just CAMERA LEFT. (Focus on a spot!)

                              CHARLES
          Mark!

     He is a bit relieved, but still tense. We hear the SOUND of a door
     closing. Charles's look is steady, fixed on Mark as Mark moves
     closer.

                              CHARLES
          What are you doing here at this hour? . . . I
          thought. . . .
                              (a pause)
          Yes, well . . . I was looking for the Clayborn
          file. . . .
                              (a pause)
          Key? . . .
                              (a nervous laugh)
          I never returned my key when I changed
          jobs. . . .
                              (adding quickly)
          Not intentionally . . . I simply forgot . . .
                              (he interrupts himself)
          Mark, why are you looking at me like that?
          We've always been friends. I'm not a criminal.
                              (listening)
          Yes, yes, I know this seems wrong . . . but
          it's for a good purpose. . . . You'll see, if I can
          find what I'm looking for. . . .
                                                  (continued)

VI (continued)

Charles turns again to the filing cabinet and digs deeper and deeper into the crowded files. He speaks while he searches:

> CHARLES (cont.)
> There's something very wrong . . .

Suddenly, he pulls out a file and turns into the CAMERA as if to get more light on the file. He is becoming more and more pleased with his findings.

> CHARLES (cont.)
> Yes! Yes! . . . Here it is. . . .
> (looking through it)
> The Osgood contracts to Mr. Clayborn. . . .

Charles turns to Mark with the good news, and finds a gun pointed in his direction. His expression changes immediately from elation to confusion.

> CHARLES (cont.)
> Mark . . .

The confusion turns to fright as Charles looks into Mark's eyes, then down at the gun (waist high) then directly into Mark's eyes again.

> CHARLES (cont.)
> Mark . . . I can't believe this . . . a gun? . . .
> What do you want? The files? . . . We're on
> the same side, aren't we? . . . Well, aren't we?
> (panic grows)
> If this information is so important . . . so
> dangerous . . . that it brings us to this . . .
> (panic builds)
> I'll give you the files and forget I ever saw
> them. . . . Don't look at me like that . . .
> Mark . . . I'll put the files back.

As Charles turns to put the file back in its place in the drawer, we hear a gun shot.

You have a choice of endings:
1. *Charles gets shot in the back and falls.*
2. *Charles freezes, then turns in Mark's direction and sees someone else at some distance away and realizes that Mark has been shot.*
3. *Create your own.*

Jean Porter during film workshop in Munich.

10

Keep It Alive!

Rarely does a modern young actor discuss his craft without a dissertation on "energy." In the context of acting, I find the word misleading, if not distasteful. Many young actors assume that energy entails an expenditure of power, and in its properly used sense, it does. But operating power is not what screen acting demands; accurately speaking, it demands more—it demands vitality.

My dictionary defines "vitality" as: "the principle of life; animation; the ability to live or capacity for lasting; continuance." All of these—let's call them "states"—are essential to the kind of acting we've been discussing.

I have learned never to ask an actor for energy. The results can be devastating. He will spit out his words, like a neophyte fresh out of RADA, breathe loudly, indulge (and this is quite common) in violent gestures or movements. But quite often, just before I say, "action," I repeat the words, "vitality, vitality." And the actor knows I am looking for life in the scene, not a volcanic explosion.

Vitality is an essential part of every performance, regardless of the mood, the pace, or the state of movement or of rest. If Camille had been lethargic as she lay dying, we would have been relieved to see her go.

A well-known pianist once remarked that it was when playing the softest tones that the greatest hand strength was required to

109

hold back the fingers while they depressed the keys sufficiently to make the soft sound. So it is with vitality. Contradictory as it may seem, a state of repose, of quiescence, even the act of quiet dying, must have life, and these two apparent opposites are quite difficult to harmonize.

The ability to produce a superabundance of vitality is probably the secret of camera presence. I hae seen actors in a state of such lethargy that they seem incapable of functioning, but once before the camera, their bodies and eyes would radiate vitality in its purest form.

Granted the indispensability of vitality, how is it acquired and how is it best exhibited or projected? As for acquisition, much of it is inborn. We all know people who are bursting with life, some from the moment they first breathe it in. Most of us are impressed by the presence of vigor in people of all ages, and we are surprised to find that such vigor is usually accompanied by a wide, open outlook on life. Vitality is partly an expression of such elasticity and quickness of mind, and partly an expression of physical health.

Most people who approach an acting career possess awareness and alertness; many, however, pay little attention to their physical condition. It is now a cliché to call an actor's body his instrument, but it is a very apt metaphor. It is through the use of the entire body that most interpersonal communication is expressed, and communication is essential in acting.*

No violinist neglects his violin. He protects it from excessive dryness, humidity, dirt, or anything else that might prevent it from producing the best possible tones. The same is true for any instrumentalist, even a harmonica player or a virtuoso on the ocharina.

All this applies to persons in other walks of life: a hunter and his instrument of death, a schusser and his skis, a baseball player and his bat and glove, a bowler and his ball, on and on and on. So why do some actors treat their bodies so carelessly? Indolence,

---

*Dogs watch their masters intently, getting more information from their owners' body attitudes and movements than they do from voice commands. No actor should be less observant than his dog.

alcohol, and drugs are hardly the means of keeping their instruments in tune.

For obvious reasons, actresses have always been more aware of the necessity for maintaining their physical appearances than have their male counterparts, but the imbalance seems to be correcting itself of late. Most actors are now quite aware of the need to shape up, but two sets of tennis on Sunday will hardly suffice. A well-planned regimen that includes exercises for stamina, strength, and agility should be high on every young actor's priority list.

Acting academies have long taught fencing for agility and grace, and it is an excellent exercise, but, like dancing and many pure sports, it requires many hours of work to do the job. (Most professional athletes now work out with weights in addition to their sports activities.)

I have always been partial to weight lifting because of its unmatched potential for over-all development and the fact that it produces maximum results rather quickly. (I am not referring to competitive lifters or Mr. Americas.) Extensive daily calisthenics, aerobics, and swimming will also do the job if they are allotted sufficient time. It is important that you choose a form of exercise that will develop all the muscles of your body. You never know when you may be called on to perform some unusual physical activity—and stunt men do not always fill the bill.

Keeping your instrument in mint condition is one thing, playing it with skill is something else. A Stradivarius in the hands of an amateur will produce more pain than melody. For the actor, as for the virtuoso, the playing is the thing. Once your body is finely tuned and you have vitality to spare, how do you get it into your performance?

By showing concern, by concentrating, by paying attention. All of these words have a very positive connotation, and they all carry the secret of vitality in acting. Like a magnifying glass that focuses scattered rays of sunlight into one bright, shining spot, concentration, by definition and by practice, brings your vitality to a common center in a greatly increased state. So pay attention, concentrate, show concern—all for the person or persons you are involved with in the scene. If you can do that with honesty, without pretense, you are well on your way to becoming an actor.

*   *   *

The actress speaks:

An actress may proudly consider herself full of energy and stamina, and run through the day's work at bonkers speed. She may show impatience when mechanical foul-ups slow the shooting of a scene, or if a fellow actor stalls or has trouble remembering a line. This kind of nervous energy is just as bad as no vitality at all. It is nerve wracking to the rest of the cast and the crew. This type of person usually clowns around a lot, which is okay for starting off the morning, but wears badly through the day.

If you have natural vitality it shows in all of your movements, controlled and disciplined. Your inner energy is present in your eyes.

It is exciting to take on another character, to become another person for a while, but it takes a lot out of you. Even a small part that works for several consecutive days can leave you drained. Acting for the screen is much more difficult than acting in the theater, for many reasons. Not the least of these is waiting. You prepare for a scene, get yourself completely worked up for whatever is expected, then you wait until everything and everyone else is ready. Usually it is best to go to your portable dressing room, keep your mind locked in on the scene to be done, and wait patiently. If the scene is easy, you might find relief in reading, crocheting, knitting, or in any time-consuming activity that demands little attention. Whatever, it is better to be alone at this point.

The first time you will feel all of your lights is when you step in front of the camera for the final rehearsal. Get to know them. Your key light will be the hottest one you will feel. For close-ups, your eye light will be very small, very close, and usually just below the camera.

During this final rehearsal you will become overly warm and you probably will perspire. Just before the first take, the director will signal the crew that he is satisfied and ready to shoot. "Okay, let's shoot it!" he'll say. At this point the makeup person and the hairdresser (who have been watching every move) will dash into the set, dab your face carefully with a makeup sponge, and rearrange a few strands of hair. Don't let this throw you. Ignore them and realize that they are there to help you. Perspiration reflects the lights, and a strand of hair can throw a shadow in the wrong place. I saw an actress throw a tantrum once, claiming this activity broke her concentration. But remember these are artists, like yourself, doing their jobs, helping your photographic image. They know you are concentrating. They won't speak to you.

Some preceding chapters contain what may appear to be a rather contradictory statement, one I feel must be clarified to make you more comfortable. We keep saying, "Forget the camera is there." This is meant to remind you to put yourself so completely into the character you are playing, and into the small setting around you, that you won't think about the camera.

But of course you know the camera is there. During this final rehearsal make certain you know where the camera is at all times. If it is to "dolly" (to move), keep in mind exactly where it will be at the moment you will be doing, or saying, a particular thing. Rehearse the scene enough to fix these points firmly in your mind. Then you can forget about the camera. Maybe.

If you are in a close or medium-close shot and your eyes are to follow a person or a car across the camera (let's say from camera left, across and past the camera, to camera right), be aware of the camera or there will be a jump. Simply imagine the object you are following goes in a straight line, right across the camera and on. Look through the camera as though it were invisible.

There may come a time when you are directed to look into the lens. This often occurs in TV sitcoms. If you are new at the game it might be a good idea to quietly ask the cameraman which part of his camera is the lens. It may not be where you think it is.

"Lights! Camera! Action!" What a beautiful phrase. If everyone loved screen acting as much as I do, we'd have little else happening.

Acting for the screen may one day be given its due credit. Because of all the careless, trite, slot-filling nonsense found on TV these days, I don't know. But there again, it has its place. There are some marvelous shows on television. Perhaps one day the networks and the advertising agencies will get together and set aside larger budgets for longer schedules, and shoot more films for TV. There is no doubt that, as a rule, the more time and money spent, the better the quality. And audiences are proving that quality counts.

But even as things are today, do your best. Get whatever roles you can, in cinema or TV, and make them noticeable. Make people remember you for what you did with a particular role.

Marlon Brando, shown here in The Young Lions, *is a perfect example of a fine actor who can put himself into any role.*

11

Don't Be With It

Acting styles change with the years. Every era has its "in" techniques. One such fashion, which started three decades ago, is still with us—naturalism. Offhand, one would think that naturalism would be a fairly simple, realistic style, but some actors won't have it that way. If it isn't "put on," overdone, it isn't acting. So naturalism, at least in some instances, has become a display of eye twitching, nose picking, and fanny scratching.

My mistake was in equating naturalism with realism, two terms that have always bothered me, since I prefer dealing in results rather than in terminology. Formal definitions indicate that as far as art is concerned they mean much the same thing; naturalism is the depiction of what is natural, or instinctive, while realism is the depiction of the natural world around us. Succinctly put, realism is showing a person in an environment where bedbugs abound; naturalism is showing that person absent-mindedly (and that's important) scratching the resultant bites.

When such natural or instinctive activity is strictly in keeping with the character's milieu, it is also real; when it is arbitrarily engaged in without regard to the environment, it is an affectation and as such, destroys the honesty and the reality of the performance.

Stylistic or affected acting has another great drawback—like any fad of the moment it doesn't age well. In clothes, an extreme style from any particular period becomes, in later years, a laughing matter or an object of curiosity. The same is true for stylistic acting.

The late 1920s and the early 1930s saw an influx of theater actors into Hollywood films; actors who brought with them the techniques then in vogue on Broadway. Today, many of the films they made demonstrate affectation in its most obvious form. One film features two actresses, one an acclaimed Broadway star, the other a product of Hollywood. The difference in styles is striking. The theater actress' speech utilizes the broad As then considered proper in her medium. Even though she is playing an middle upper-class midwestern woman, her training demanded that she speak with an accent that William Wellman once described as "Kansas City British." It was neither real nor natural, but the style was "in."

The film actress, on the other hand, spoke clean-cut, midwestern American, a manner of speech with few affectations. From today's point of view, the theater actress' performance looks false, while the film actress' is true, and will probably remain so for some time to come. The scenes in which they appear are colored by their acting styles; those of one seem cleverly contrived, while those of the other still carry the feeling of reality.

Most artists would like to believe that, contrary to Marc Antony's pronouncement, the good that they do will live after them. For all artists that means presenting, whether in painting, in literature, or in films, the essence of human thought and behavior. As every student of history knows, this has changed little over hundreds of years. We still find truth and enjoyment in *Oliver Twist* and *Huckleberry Finn*.

When acting is founded on the basic ethical and moral attitudes of humankind (and on their typical imperfections), they remain dramatically effective through generations of time. This does not mean that the foibles, tastes in dress, and behavior of any particular period cannot be depicted on the screen (in fact, they usually are), but that they should be, as they are in life, purely surface phenomena laid over the solid base of long-lasting, essential human nature.

Errors in these areas are most often seen in the perpetuation of the stereotype and in the use of archaic or exotic language. As mentioned earlier, we have no working knowledge of common speech of the past since we have only the literary presentation of their speech habits. But the poetry of Chaucer or of Shakespeare mirrored the conversational speech of the man in the street no more accurately than the poetry of Dylan Thomas mirrors the common speech of today. One of King Arthur's knights might have said, "Gadzooks!" or "Ho, varlet!", but unless you're looking for laughs, you should no more use such words in depicting a man of the Middle Ages than you would pepper the speech of a grandfather type with "twenty-three skiddoo," or "you're the bee's knees." Asking an actor who is playing Marco Polo to use modern colloquialisms (which has been done) is as unforgivable as asking a modern hipster to declaim with the rhetoric of Winston Churchill.

The safe approach is to avoid semantic excesses, whether you are using the jargon of a truck driver or a college professor (though either one can, at times, speak like the other). The same guidelines serve in the presentation of a character, except in broad comedy, where exaggeration is the nature of things. But for relatively straight characterization, it is wise to remember a line from Robert Burns: "A man is a man for a'that." No matter what the cultural surface coating of a character, whether it be as extreme as the eighteenth-century simpering of a member of the royal court, or the sour demeanor of a late nineteenth-century moralist, we are all brothers under the skin. Remembering that will give your characterizations "legs" and longevity.

*   *   *

The actress speaks:

Why is acting one of our most desired careers? Escape? Acting allows you to get out of yourself and become another person. Power? While acting you can hold an entire audience and manipulate them as you please. Money? I do hope it isn't for the money, but as of late, screen actors' salaries are astronomical. You want to be loved? If you're not loved by someone already, acting won't help you.

To every beginner who dreams of becoming a movie star, I just want to tell you, it can be done. It takes time, a long time. It takes patience, a great deal of patience. It takes persistence and hard work, lots of it. If you don't have the kind of character and personality to put forth, and put up with, all of these things, you probably won't make it. But if you believe you have the talent, the heart and the strength to pursue—pursue! The rewards are worth the effort.

Look in the mirror. Are you beautiful? Gorgeous? Handsome? Pretty? Pretty good looking? Attractive? Which? Gotta be in there somewhere.

You must be photogenic for the screen. You must have good facial bone structure, and your eyes, nose, and mouth must be interesting, if not appealing. To be luscious is perfect, but we can't have it all. If you know you have an abundance of sex appeal, that helps. Your skin should be clear of all blemishes, so keep it clean and watch your diet.

To be of lasting importance on the screen you must have a healthy and attractive body. The camera adds ten pounds, so a woman must always keep her weight down. While you're young, that's easy, so start now and keep the good habits. One of the easiest ways to decrease in weight and inches is to simply eat half portions of what you have been eating. If you get hungry between meals, have a tablespoon of honey or a small piece of jack cheese and a cracker (just one). If you keep to this you'll be proud of yourself and will enjoy being asked, "How do you do it?"

Exercise is a must, but in today's world everyone is so aware of this that I probably don't need to carry on about it. I would like to say that for a woman's body, dancing is the most important exercise. It gives you rhythm, grace, charm, and style. Dancing helps you to develop easy, subtle, sexy body movements, with or without music.

Once you make up your mind that cinema/TV is the career you are choosing, write down your goals. Put them right there in front of you. Plan your work and work your plan. Prepare yourself in every way you can, then go to it. Once you start, don't give up. You may need to change course several times during your training, your amateur try-outs, and your planning, but remember that's as it should be. You may start out playing comedy and discover you can do other things. Changes mean you are growing. But if you make a change and don't like it, go back to what you are comfortable with. No matter what, always be honest with yourself.

Most of us start out in school plays. Encouraged by audience response, we believe we have a future in acting. It's easy to go on to the next step and get into local community little theater groups. Every town has at least one. Again, encouraged by good audience reaction and backed by a belief in yourself, you move on. By this time you should move to where the real action is. If you choose theater, your move will probably be to the nearest city with a good, nationally recognized theater, your ultimate aim being Broadway, of course.

If you choose screen acting, you will head for Hollywood; it is still the center for filmmaking, and it always will be. New York has a lot of television production, but Hollywood has it all. Sure, films are shot all across the nation, but basically, the center is here. Tinseltown, the Filmworld, takes the brunt of all the sad jokes made by those who fail and leave. They find fault with the place if they're unsuccessful. No need to do that. It will survive, and you may be back.

The first thing you have to do after arriving in L.A. is to get some attention. (Don't rob a bank!) This will take some time, so you should bring enough money to carry you through four seasons, or you will have to get an earthling job of some sort to sustain you. There are always waiter and waitress jobs available.

Get acquainted. From a newstand, pick up the trade papers (Hollywood Reporter and Variety) to find out what's going on in all the studios. Here you can also take note of which agents are getting jobs for what actors. Study these. Learn to remember the names of agents and casting directors.

Find out where fellow actors and actresses hang out and go there. Listen to everybody and get to know them. Let them know you are a likable person and no threat. Make friends.

Get an agent. If you have guts, and you do have guts or you wouldn't be here, you will get an agent. As an unknown, you won't expect the top agents in town to be waiting for your call, but there are all kinds of agents, and there are all kinds of legitimate ways of getting one. Sift through all the information you will pick up here an there and choose for yourself the best way to go about it.

Prove your ability to your agent. If you've only done school plays and little theater he probably will suggest that you get into some screen acting classes and do some show-cases where *casting directors go to view scenes played by promising new-comers. These show-cases are advertised in the trade papers and in* Drama-Logue. *Also watch for announcements from local universities or the American Film Institute. They advertise coming film production, and interviews are set up to choose actors and actresses for key roles. These student films are good experience and will give you film to show in future job hunting.*

If you see in the Hollywood Reporter *production chart that Gem-Stone Productions Co. is preparing* Do it My Way, *and you happened to have seen it on the stage and consider yourself perfect for the supporting role of Marcia Mae, look to see who the casting director is, phone the company, and ask for an appointment. (This is if you have no agent.) Don't be bashful. Don't be rude, either. Just give it a try. Who knows? You might get an appointment. If you can't get one by phone, go over to the production company and leave your photo and résumé with a note asking for an interview. Be clever. Make them want to see you. If that part is taken, maybe you'll get something else. Don't settle for nothing.*

Remember all the while, and this covers a lot of time, you will be meeting people and becoming known. If people like you they will help you. You can't get anywhere in this town if you are disliked. Let people know, graciously, that you need help, and when given it, be grateful. Show-biz people like to give a hand, but they also like to know it's been appreciated; not by the buck, but by sincere warmth and continued friendship. When you get your first break, you'll want to give a party!

Postscript

To whom it may concern

Norman Cousins said, "We are turning out young men and women . . . who are beautifully skilled but intellectually underdeveloped."* Mikhail Baryshnikov speaks about the absence of strong personalities among performing artists today: "It's a sociological problem for all of us, not just dancers but actors and musicians too. We are a lost generation, a lot of people who are aggressive and virtuosic but who have little inside. Some ask, 'Where's the beef?' I ask, 'Where's the soul?'

"Today's young performers have to get more cultural language, more exposure and education. They must learn how to project real feelings, to be real people. Being an artist in the biggest sense comes down to being a *mensch*."**

Baryshnikov's prescription is deceptively simple; filling it seems to be very difficult indeed. Observing, listening, reading, are essential but hardly enough. The key is "real feelings . . . real people." That means getting beneath the beauty (or the ugliness) of the skin to the person below. Surface manifestations give us

---

*Editorial, *Saturday Review*. May/June 1983.
**Los Angeles *Times*, March 22, 1984. Interview with Donna Perlmutter.

a picture, they do not give us art. A brief flash of truth touches us infinitely more deeply than an hour of virtuosity. Jean and I recently saw a film in which two well-known actors ranted, raved, and gesticulated, all quite skillfully, and we felt we were watching contortionists at work—virtuosic and interesting to look at but hardly worth taking to one's heart. A short while before we had seen a film clip—three short close-ups from *Casablanca*—in which Bogart and Bergman look at each other. That's it. No words, no gestures, no tricks—they just *look* at each other. But Jean and I both sobbed involuntarily at the sheer beauty of the scene. Because, in the entire art of acting, nothing is more beautiful than honesty and truth presented with utter simplicity.

Filmography of the Authors

Edward Dmytryk

THE HAWK   (Ind)   (1935)
TELEVISION SPY   (Para)   (1939)
EMERGENCY SQUAD   (Para)   (1939)
GOLDEN GLOVES   (Para)   (1939)
MYSTERY SEA RAIDER   (Para)   (1940)
HER FIRST ROMANCE   (I.E. Chadwick)   (1940)
THE DEVIL COMMANDS   (Col)   (1940)
UNDER AGE   (Col)   (1940)
SWEETHEART OF THE CAMPUS   (Col)   (1941)
THE BLONDE FROM SINGAPORE   (Col)   (1941)
SECRETS OF THE LONE WOLF   (Col)   (1941)
CONFESSIONS OF BOSTON BLACKIE   (Col)   (1941)
COUNTER-ESPIONAGE   (Col)   (1942)
SEVEN MILES FROM ALCATRAZ   (RKO)   (1942)
HITLER'S CHILDREN   (RKO)   (1943)
THE FALCON STRIKES BACK   (RKO)   (1943)
CAPTIVE WILD WOMAN   (Univ)   (1943)
BEHIND THE RISING SUN   (RKO)   (1943)
TENDER COMRADE   (RKO)   1943)
MURDER, MY SWEET   (RKO)   (1944)

BACK TO BATAAN   (RKO)   (1945)
CORNERED   (RKO)   (1945)
TILL THE END OF TIME   (RKO)   (1945)
SO WELL REMEMBERED   (RKO-RANK)   (1946)
CROSSFIRE   (RKO)   (1947)
THE HIDDEN ROOM   (English Ind.)   (1948)
GIVE US THIS DAY   (Eagle-Lion)   (1949)
MUTINY   (King Bros.-U.A.)   (1951)
THE SNIPER   (Kramer-Col)   (1951)
EIGHT IRON MEN   (Kramer-Col)   (1952)
THE JUGGLER   (Kramer-Col)   (1952)
THE CAINE MUTINY   (Kramer-Col)   (1953)
BROKEN LANCE   (20th-Fox)   (1954)
THE END OF THE AFFAIR   (Col)   (1954)
SOLDIER OF FORTUNE   (20th-Fox)   (1955)
THE LEFT HAND OF GOD   (20th-Fox)   (1955)
THE MOUNTAIN   (Para)   (1956)
RAINTREE COUNTY   (MGM)   (1956)
THE YOUNG LIONS   (20th-Fox)   (1957)
WARLOCK   (20th-Fox)   (1958)
THE BLUE ANGEL   (20th-Fox)   (1959)
WALK ON THE WILD SIDE   (Col)   (1961)
THE RELUCTANT SAINT   (Col)   (1961)
THE CARPETBAGGERS   (Para)   (1963)
WHERE LOVE HAS GONE   (Para)   (1964)
MIRAGE   (Univ)   (1965)
ALVAREZ KELLY   (Col)   (1966)
ANZIO   (Col)   (1967)
SHALAKO   (Cinerama)   (1968)
BLUEBEARD   (Cinerama)   (1972)
THE HUMAN FACTOR   (Bryanston)   (1975)

Jean Porter Dmytryk

Film

SONG AND DANCE MAN   (20th C-Fox)   (1935)
TOM SAWYER   (David O. Selznick Prod.)   (1936)
HEART OF THE RIO GRANDE   (Republic)   (1937)
HELLZAPOPPIN'   (Univ)   (1937)
SAN FERNANDO VALLEY   (Republic)   (1938)
THE UNDER PUP   (Univ)   (1938)
STRIKE UP THE BAND   (MGM)   (1939)
HENRY ALDRICH FOR PRESIDENT   (Para)   (1939)
ONE MILLION B.C.   (Hal Roach)   (1939)
BABES ON BROADWAY   (MGM)   (1940)
KISS THE BOYS GOODBYE   (Paramount)   (1940)
ABOUT FACE   (Hal Roach)   (1940)
FALL IN   (Hal Roach)   (1940)
NASTY NUISANCE   (Hal Roach)   (1941)
CALABOOSE   (Hal Roach)   (1941)
THE YOUNGEST PROFESSION   (MGM)   (1942)
ANDY HARDY'S BLONDE TROUBLE   (MGM)   (1942)
YOUNG IDEAS   (MGM)   (1943)
BATHING BEAUTY   (MGM)   (1943)
ABBOT AND COSTELLO IN HOLLYWOOD
    (MGM)   (1944)
EASY TO WED   (MGM)   (1945)
WHAT NEXT, CORPORAL HARGROVE   (MGM)   (1945)
TILL THE END OF TIME   (RKO)   (1946)
BETTY CO-ED   (Col)   (1946)
SWEET GENEVIEVE   (Col)   (1947)
TWO BLONDES AND A REDHEAD   (Col)   (1947)
LITTLE MISS BROADWAY   (Col)   (1947)
THAT HAGEN GIRL   (Warner Bros.)   (1948)
CRY DANGER   (RKO)   (1949)
KENTUCKY JUBILEE   (Lippert Prod.)   (1950)
G.I. JANE   (Lippert Prod.)   (1950)
RACING BLOOD   (Independent)   (1950)
THE LEFT HAND OF GOD   (RKO)   (1955)

Television

A regular on the RED SKELTON COMEDY HOUR
   (1954-1955)
A regular in the ABBOT AND COSTELLO FILMS
   made for TV   (1945-1946)
Live TV   HALLMARK THEATER   (CBS)   (1955)
Live TV   NINETY MINUTES   (CBS)   (1956)
Live TV   ODYSSEY   (CBS Special)   (1957)
Guest Star on many TV weekly shows